Praise for

"Bernadette Smith's approach to inclusion offers strategies for every department. Read this book, put it into practice, and then share it with everyone you know."

JENNIFER BROWN,
FOUNDER AND CEO, JENNIFER BROWN CONSULTING.
AUTHOR OF HOW TO BE AN INCLUSIVE LEADER

"Diversity is meaningless without true inclusion. What matters is changing the systems and being a consistent ally. This book shows you a clear path on how to be a supportive ally and change agent."

JASMINE E. GUY,
DIRECTOR OF DIVERSITY, EQUITY, AND INCLUSION AND CORPORATE
SOCIAL RESPONSIBILITY, MAJOR, LINDSEY & AFRICA

"This book is the definitive guide for any organization just beginning their diversity, equity, and inclusion journey. Full of practical advice and inspirational ideas, Inclusive 360 helps you move from theory to action."

DREW STERN,
COO, NETWORK VENTURES

"Inclusive 360 is a fully customizable blueprint to set you on your path towards a truly inclusive organization. From the front line to the executive team, everyone should read this book."

SCOTT Y. STUART,
CEO, TURNAROUND MANAGEMENT ASSOCIATION

"The book's illuminating message is honest, forthright, and timely.
An aspirational and well-grounded management guide."

KIRKUS REVIEWS

"This DEI guide from one of the industry's best is an invaluable, empowering, and educational resource. I'm endorsing the author's aptitude in this space as well as her practical Inclusive 360 which moves you from theory to action."

CHERIE PRICE COLEMAN,
PRESIDENT, ILLINOIS DIVERSITY COUNCIL

"The data and stories are great, and I really love the hands-on practical advice in the book. It provides a lot of prompts and tools to pick from for a DEI committee. It also enables the group to look at all potential areas to work on and pick specific ones to prioritize and start with."

NATASHA MILLER WILLIAMS,
VP, HEAD OF DIVERSITY, EQUITY, AND INCLUSION, FERRARA

"Diversity and inclusion is more important than ever, and we all should be taking more action to create a more united society for us and generations to come. Bernadette Smith is the leader to listen to when you're intimidated by diversity. This practical, passionate, and relatable book will make the work of creating truly inclusive organizations seem simpler than you may expect."

RUBÉN ALEJANDRO RAMÍREZ,
HEAD DIVERSITY AND INCLUSION, SYNGENTA GROUP

"If you're grappling with how to advance your workplace's DEI commitments, then check out Inclusive 360. The book offers a trusted blueprint with practical and actionable strategies. When you follow it, your organization will be better positioned to give each of your colleagues what they need so that they can do their best work."

RHODES PERRY,
FOUNDER & CEO OF RHODES PERRY CONSULTING,
AND BEST-SELLING AUTHOR OF BELONGING AT WORK

"Looking for the next step on your journey to create a more inclusive workplace? Be sure to read Inclusive 360. It contains an outstanding collection of real-life examples from organizations across many industries, with a step-by-step approach to identifying what you can do to make your workplace more diverse, inclusive, and successful."

**KAREN CATLIN,
AUTHOR OF BETTER ALLIES**

"Understanding diverse team members and clients and how best to serve them is the key to driving your business success. This is a fast-paced, wise, witty, practical, and helpful book by Bernadette Smith."

**DERRICK M. JOHNSON II,
CHIEF DIVERSITY OFFICER & DIRECTOR OF EVENT STRATEGY,
TALLEY MANAGEMENT GROUP**

"By now, we all know the benefits of an inclusive culture and the impact on productivity, profitability, innovation and creativity. Inclusive 360 provides a customizable roadmap to set you on the path towards a truly inclusive organization. Wherever you are in your inclusion practice, this book offers insights and best practices to move you forward."

**JACKIE FERGUSON,
CERTIFIED DIVERSITY EXECUTIVE, CO-FOUNDER OF THE DIVERSITY
MOVEMENT, MEMBER OF THE NATIONAL DIVERSITY COUNCIL AND THE
FORBES BUSINESS COUNCIL**

"As a C-level, gay woman working in tech for 20+ years, diversity is meaningless without true inclusion. Change can be difficult, but it's worth it. It's not only important to the success of your business, but the success of your team, your fellow humans. Representation matters and leadership, leads. It starts at the top and means changing the systems, supporting personal journeys, and being a consistent ally. This book shows you a clear path on how to do just that."

**COLLEEN D. EGAN,
CEO, ILLINOIS SCIENCE AND TECHNOLOGY COALITION**

Inclusive

360

Proven Solutions
for an Equitable
Organization

by Bernadette Smith

Published by Goodnow Flow Publishing.
First printing, September 21, 2021.

First Edition

Books may be purchased in bulk for promotional, educational, or business use. For more information, contact your local bookseller or by email at info@theequalityinstitute.com

Library of Congress Control Number: 2021915090

ISBN: 978-1-7376354-3-7 (hc)
ISBN: 978-1-7376354-1-3 (pbk)
ISBN: 978-1-7376354-2-0 (epub)

Printed in the United States of America.
Book designed by Ian Berg
Headshot by John A. DeMato

Dedication:

For everyone who strives for a world where
we are not judging each other for who we are
and who we are not. For Patrick, Olivia, Eve,
Tessa, Scarlett, and all other kids for whom
I'm committed to leaving the world better
than I found it.

I won't let you down.

Table of Contents

Foreword

IT WAS EARLY August 1994, and the much-anticipated letter finally arrived in the mail, detailing my freshman year dorm assignment: Boston University Warren Towers, Room 1119C. And most importantly: a roommate named Bernadette Smith.

Bernadette and I talked on the phone a few days later, and we stumbled through small talk about our summer jobs and favorite music. Eventually, we made all the critical decisions: Yes, we'll rent a microfridge. No, we don't need a TV. Sure, let's sign up for this new thing called dial-up internet.

Once we moved in, hung our posters, and stuffed our tiny freezer with ice pops, any awkwardness between us vanished. Bernadette and I share a love of whimsy, so we covered the ceiling with sheets of wrapping paper and our door with random stickers we found around campus. We recorded silly outgoing messages on the answering machine, sometimes together, but sometimes to shock the other person. We both longed to feel part of the community, so I took a part-time job teaching swim lessons to recent immigrants to Boston, and Bernadette founded a chapter of Habitat for Humanity.

In those early days, we spent most of our days apart, immersed in activities, clubs, classes, and new friendships. At night, though, we had a ritual: listening to a bedtime mixtape we compiled during our first week together. Sometimes, one of us would drift off before the end of the first song (Lisa Loeb's Stay–a song that will forever transport me back to 1994 and my plaid flannel sheets). But more often, the start of the tape would initiate deep conversation, held in the dark until one of us succumbed to exhaustion. No topic felt off-limits. We shared stories, giggled, and unpacked everything from toxic high school relationships to our opinions about the death penalty.

Boston University put us together in that little cinderblock-walled room, probably the result of a random lottery. It turned out to be a decision that changed my outlook on friendship... and informed my behaviors for years to come.

Shortly before Thanksgiving Break, a mutual friend asked me to join him and Bernadette for a conversation in our room. Bernadette sat on her bed, holding a pink pillow, looking anxious. I silently took a seat on my bed, also anxious. The three of us stared at each other, at the floor, and at nothing at all.

Bernadette eventually broke the silence. "I'm a lesbian," she said.

Bernadette found the courage to share her truth a month earlier, on October 11–National Coming Out Day. Because our 110 square foot room provided no opportunity for privacy, she'd been fabricating excuses for why she was gone at times. My participation in a campus band on Monday afternoons coincided with BU's LGB Association meetings, so that night wasn't difficult. On Thursday nights, when a local club provided a gay-friendly hangout space, Bernadette had been pretending to be at the library.

Bernadette didn't want to lie to me anymore, even if it changed things between us.

I'm sure my face couldn't hide my horror, but not for any of the reasons she feared. Bernadette's sexuality didn't matter to me at all, but something about our relationship gave her the impression that it may.

Even at 18 and without a fully developed frontal cortex, I knew I would never intentionally make anyone feel unwelcome or unsafe. At that moment, with the three of us awkwardly navigating this conversation, I had to face the hard truth that I had said or done something that caused Bernadette to wait nearly a month to tell me.

That's the thing about blind spots. By definition, they don't exist in our consciousness until they do. And then they are so obvious that we are shocked, appalled, aghast. We either respond with anger or vow to do things differently in the future.

Bernadette's coming-out story is hers to tell. My only part of her story is that it changed me. I've done a lot of things differently since then.

That's exactly why this book exists. It exposes blind spots you don't even know you have. Without judgment, it offers tangible suggestions for overcoming them.

Leadership is not a title. Leadership is action. Business consultants will say that no matter your position in your company, you can make a difference. You can speak up when you feel injustice. You can ensure that all voices are heard around the table. You can advocate for policies that foster a welcoming, inclusive, and productive environment. Be the change you want to see, we are told.

I challenge you to go one step further. Regardless of your position within your company – from entry-level staff members to the CEO– you don't simply have the ability to be the change. You have an obligation to do so.

I lead an organization that is dedicated to telling the stories of women who make our world a better place. The enduring value of the National Women's Hall of Fame's inductees cannot be understated: they are women with breath-taking contributions in their fields, ranging from science to politics. Too many of these stories include examples of how these incredible women overcame hostile environments and watched as their accomplishments were stolen, diminished, or forgotten. We use their perseverance as inspiration for our own lives and for our commitment to promote equality, regardless of gender, class, age, skin color, or sexuality.

Your business may be in any stage of understanding the importance of inclusive policies and practices to the success of your endeavor. No matter where you are at, these pages offer a path forward. Bernadette shares real examples and tangible tips that you will find easily adaptable. In the process, you will bring more people into the core of your mission and exponentially increase your possibilities of success.

Great leaders and mentors teach us that learning never ends. For me, that realization began in Warren Towers, Room 1119C, and a roommate named Bernadette Smith.

I'm so excited to be able to share her with you.

Jennifer S Gabriel
EXECUTIVE DIRECTOR,
NATIONAL WOMEN'S HALL OF FAME.

Introduction

I'M BERNADETTE SMITH and I'm a keynote speaker, author, and owner of a consulting firm called Equality Institute that address-es **diversity, equity, and inclusion** (DEI). A few years ago, I spent the day at a DEI summit in Chicago, where I live. On the walk back to the train I began reflecting on some of my takeaways from the event, and thought, "my mom was right—you do learn something new every day!"

I decided right then and there, on a sidewalk in Chicago, to make a short selfie video, sharing what I learned. I tagged it #1ThingILearned-Today and uploaded it to LinkedIn. I was terrified, but I did it anyway.

The next day I did it again. I kept doing it every weekday and over time, I added closed captions (because that's truly inclusive) and decid-ed to get specific about my goals for the videos.

I've always been an optimist. I can't help it. It's baked into me. Even on the roller coaster ride of entrepreneurship, I never stay down for long. I realized that if these little #1ThingILearnedToday videos were to be truly authentic, they had to be positive. I committed to only shar-ing what I considered to be good news, or best practices, exclusively re-lated to diversity, equity, inclusion, or corporate social responsibility.

I soon discovered that it's much easier to find negative news to share. There's no shortage of data or stories about institutions wronging oth-ers or the environment. But digging a little deeper, I discovered that there's also no shortage of stories about people and institutions doing truly inspiring work. That's what I sought to share: inspiration.

My goal for the videos was simple: once a week, I would hope one person watches a video and thinks, "Wow, that's really cool." That's it. A tiny nugget of inspiration, of hope.

One of my favorite quotes is from Robert F. Kennedy:

> *"Each time a man stands up for an ideal, or acts to improve the lot of others, or strikes out against injustice, he sends forth a tiny ripple of hope, and crossing each other from a million different centers of energy and daring, those ripples build a current which can sweep down the mightiest walls of oppression and resistance."* [1]

Maybe the stories I share send out a tiny ripple of hope.

A few months into this project, I committed to spreading that hope beyond the people who saw the #1ThingILearnedToday videos. Now each Saturday morning, a week's worth of good news and best practices goes out in my eNewsletter. I named it 5 Things: Bringing Good Vibes to DEI.

I regularly receive comments like the following. They fill me up and keep me going: *Grateful for your '5 Things' good vibe emails over the last year. They helped guide me through challenging conversations with my team and provided a light in some dark times.*

Join us at
TheEqualityInstitute.com/join
if you'd like a weekly dose of inspiration.

When the COVID-19 pandemic arrived, I hit my maximum bandwidth and the videos stopped, but the stories and the newsletter remained. Those stories have become this, my fourth book.

I've written this book to create those ripples of hope, to build those currents which can sweep down the mightiest walls of oppression and resistance. I'm ready to share a solutions-oriented, systemic approach to organizational inclusion.

I'm going to keep showing up and sharing. Are you?

Who this book is for

This book is packed with ideas, particularly for organizations beginning their diversity, equity, and inclusion journeys. While leaders of more established DEI programs will find plenty of value as well, many of the initiatives discussed in this book are already used by the most progressive large-scale organizations.

Perhaps you're on the new DEI Task Force at a growing tech company that only has 250 employees, but expects to quadruple their employees in the next two years. This is a great time to build strong, sustainable, and scalable DEI systems. This book will help you do that.

Perhaps you're the first DEI employee at your company and are looking for a roadmap to help build out the systems. This book will be your roadmap.

Maybe you work for a mid-sized company that only has the diversity training required by compliance and hasn't made any real progress towards DEI. This book will tell you where to begin.

Maybe you're a leader of a **Business Resource Group** and are looking for some good ideas to propose to your Executive Sponsor. This book will be your guide.

Inclusive 360 will help all of you.

Who this book is not for

This book is not for the people who are looking for a quick fix to DEI. There is none.

This book is also not for the people who are looking for a lot of "how." While the book is full of ideas, in many cases, you'll have to figure out how to implement them within your own organization. The policy changes outlined in this book are not one-size-fits-all.

You'll have to adapt your approach to find the right fit for your own organization.

I'm American, and my book is admittedly quite American-centric. The concepts are certainly transferable to wherever you are but the laws, data, and specific resources may not be.

And while "inclusion" is for all, this book should not be your go-to guide when it comes to including people with disabilities. There are some ideas in each section for ways to support and include people with disabilities, but to be truly inclusive of them, you'll also need to look at the annual guidelines for American with Disabilities Act (**ADA**) compliance.[2]

What does it mean to be Inclusive 360?

First of all, *Inclusive 360* is not about 360-degree performance reviews!

Traditional DEI efforts are focused on human resources or leadership. *Inclusive 360* takes a holistic and systemic approach to DEI by addressing not just human resources and leadership strategies, but strategies for every department.

Organizations that are *Inclusive 360* live their values not only with their employees, but also with their customers and suppliers. True inclusion requires a multi-layered approach that should touch every person within the organization.

Organizations that take an active, consistent *Inclusive 360* approach are also likely antiracist. **Antiracism** is a concept I'll explore more in Chapter 7, but to summarize, it's the consistent practice of dismantling systems of racism and making up for previous racial injustice and inequity. Many employees want to work at organizations that are proactively antiracist.

Becoming *Inclusive 360* is not a one-and-done, but this book will provide you with clear ideas that will move every department of your organization forward towards justice.

How to use this book

I'm a practical person and, admittedly, not a very process-oriented person. I'm a results-oriented person. I'm a solutions-oriented person. But I'm not going to lie: authentic DEI work requires that you roll up your sleeves and engage in the process. It requires difficult conversations. It requires vulnerability and humility. Are you that kind of leader?

This book is all about providing concrete solutions to today's most pressing DEI problems. You'll find many great ideas in the pages to come, so grab your favorite instrument and get ready to take notes as you go. Each chapter begins by identifying some pressing DEI *problems*, then provides *solutions* implemented by today's leading brands. Finally, each chapter wraps up with some suggested *actions* your organization can begin to implement.

Throughout the chapters, you'll see **bolded** words–these words are defined for you in the glossary at the end of the book.

Each mini case study you'll read has been implemented in other organizations and has proven successful. In many cases, the little stories will shed light on how to set these policies in place and will provide you with enough information to get you started. As you move into implementation mode, use the resources mentioned in the book, such as partner agencies, consulting firms, media, and more to supplement *Inclusive 360*.

This book is divided into three primary sections: Diversity, Equity, and Inclusion, with one concluding chapter on the holy grail of the workplace: **Belonging**. Each of the first three sections can be read as a standalone section, but I'd recommend that you read the book in order. I'd also advise you not to take major action until you've finished the book. If you're anything like me, you're going to read a fabulous idea from one of these chapters and want to take immediate action. My advice is to slow down. You'll need some time and support in order to most effectively implement your chosen strategies.

This book has many ideas, so I'd suggest you read it with a group of people, such as a DEI Council, people in the C-Suite, or other key stakeholders. This way you can each take note of the ideas that seem like "quick wins" and make plans to set in motion some of the ideas that require long-term planning. You may find that everyone has different priorities, but to make any of these initiatives stick, you'll need a group of stakeholders to buy-in.

Once you finish this book and decide on strategies, I encourage you to implement ideas from each section simultaneously. For example, don't make your way through the diversity section before you start implementing ideas from the inclusion section. If you don't offer an inclusive work environment, then your employees, especially the diverse, **underrepresented** ones you've just worked so hard to attract, are more likely to leave. You need inclusion to leverage the power of diversity, a recurring theme you may notice in this book. Some things may not work for your organization, and that's OK. This book is full of ideas, and you may have to test a variety of them out to find the best fit. Most organizations are good at trying new things—that's how innovation occurs. Do not despair if you try an idea from this book and it doesn't quite fit your organization. Try something else! Keep going.

As you move into solutions-mode, consider which ideas can be quick wins? Which ideas will have a direct impact on the organization's business objectives? Which ideas require external support? Will some of these ideas cost you money? Of course. Will they save you money in employee turnover? Of course. Will they improve your brand's image? Of course. These strategies are not a "get inclusion quick" scheme, but they are systemic changes, and if you follow this roadmap, you will find that your company culture will shift into a profitable culture of inclusion.

So, if you're ready to shift your culture and truly become *Inclusive 360*, let's jump in!

Part 1:
DIVERSITY

CHAPTER 1

Walk this Way

Understand your why

THINK DEEPLY ABOUT your socialization process, the messages you received growing up, the communities you live in today, the company you keep, the books you read, and the music you listen to. How have those things affected your own lived experiences? Your own **biases**?

This work is hard and, admittedly, this work may challenge those (like me!) who are results oriented. This work requires reflection, vulnerability, curiosity, and openness. It requires you to locate yourself and find your reason to make this meaningful, your reason to do this right.

Are you ready?

Start with WHY.

That's the theme of Simon Sinek's legendary TED Talk and book. He argues that customers, clients, and employees aren't interested in what you do, but why you do it. What's your purpose? As an organization. As an individual. *Sell that.*

Your WHY is your North Star. Your WHY will give you a reason to show up, put in the work, and have tough conversations to advance diversity, equity, and inclusion within your organization.

So, what is your WHY? Why does your work matter? Why are you invested?

- Is it because you realize you have **privilege** and want to pay it forward?
- Is it because someone mentored you back in the day, and you want to pay it forward?
- Is it because you believe in the purpose of your organization and want to see it thrive?
- Is it because you believe these initiatives will ultimately create a better future for your kids?

Have a clear understanding of your WHY before you continue. You need to know WHY you're doing this and what impact you hope to make in your life and the lives of those around you.

As an organization begins its diversity, equity, and inclusion journey, it must be clear on its own WHY. That WHY must be communicated from senior leadership to every person in the organization. Over, and over, and over again. Perhaps the WHY is part of the organization's core values. Perhaps it's deeply personal to senior leadership, as it is to Tim Cook, who is the openly gay CEO of Apple, or as it is to Lowe's CEO Marvin Ellison, who happens to be Black.

WHY? I'll tell you mine.

For 15 years, I ran a business that specialized in planning weddings for couples who identified as lesbian, gay, bisexual, or **transgender**. The goal was to support these couples and allow them to feel safe and free from discrimination when planning their wedding. As I worked with couples, I witnessed them at their most vulnerable and raw moments, and what I learned has defined my career in the years since.

Back in 2010, I had a client named Joanne. Joanne and I worked very closely together while I was planning her wedding. She impacted me so dramatically because she was not just any bride —Joanne is transgender.

Joanne came out to me as transgender the first time we met. She was very clear in telling me that she wanted me to help her "be the bride she'd always dreamed of."

No pressure!

Working with Joanne, I was with her at her most vulnerable. Throughout our time together, Joanne shared her fears with me—and there were many, justifiably so. She was afraid of experiencing discrimination with every vendor with whom we spoke. She was insecure about her body and appearance in a dress. She was afraid of being misgendered when we were going to appointments. She was anxious about her family's involvement and participation in the wedding. She had concerns about her transgender friends' experiences in the restroom at the wedding venue.

Joanne's fears became my responsibility because I was her planner. Not only that—I was also her advocate. I had her back. It was my responsibility to make sure she had nothing to be afraid of. It was my responsibility to preemptively communicate with those people we considered hiring for the wedding. It was my responsibility to ensure there were all-gender restrooms on site. Although I couldn't do anything regarding her family's involvement, I listened with compassion as she talked through her concerns.

I also learned that, before we started working together, her employer forced Joanne out of her job when she came out as transgender. She was a high-powered executive who had to take a lower paying job elsewhere. At the time, there were no protections against employment discrimination towards someone who was transgender in her state. She had no recourses against her employer except to move on.

Before meeting Joanne, all of the weddings I'd planned were for **cisgender LGBTQ** couples, and sure, they had plenty of concerns about coming out, family acceptance and discrimination—but those couples didn't have the added fears shared by Joanne.

Little did Joanne know that our time together would come to shape my career. In Joanne, I rediscovered my "WHY."

In Joanne, I was reminded that I was put on this earth to make a difference. I am here to help those who are at risk of bias feel safe. To work to ensure all are treated fairly by the people they encounter and can go about their lives with dignity. I was reminded that I have unique talents and the ability to communicate with others in a way that helps them "get it" without feeling judged.

Joanne wrote a book to help others understand the lives of transgender people, and in my copy inscribed the following, *"With profound thanks for helping me be the bride I always wanted to be."*

Ironically, I am the grateful one. In the years since we worked together, I still sometimes forget my WHY, but as I wrote this, I printed out a small photo from her wedding and hung it on my office corkboard. This will continue to remind me of my WHY on a daily basis.

This book is not all about Joanne, the topic of transgender people, or LGBTQ issues. It is about the importance of diversity, equity, and inclusion and how they show up in the workplace. The rules have changed and my goal in this book is to show you the path forward.

Although I'm cisgender, I've learned how to be an **ally** to Joanne and plenty of others. I've learned how to use my voice and my way of communicating to help those who are "othered" in any way.

The goal of this book is to give you a clear path forward while creating lots of win-wins—for the employee, for the organization, and for all consumers.

It's easier than you think but it starts with changing the rules. Changing the systems.

"Even when people have positive intentions, you have to make it clear and easy for them to make inclusive decisions by embedding it in everyday processes and communications. For example, when hiring, you have to make it an explicit expectation that managers proactively build more diverse networks, and then build it into reward mechanisms. If you want executives to talk about diversity, you have to make it a standing agenda item tied to business goals, and give them regular visibility into how they're doing. It cannot be a side project. It can't just be at the diversity meeting. And it can't just come from the same person." [3]

CANDICE MORGAN, PARTNER AT GOOGLE VENTURES.

Make the case

According to the Center for Talent Innovation (now Coqual), more than one-third of Black employees intend to leave their companies within two years, and Black professionals are 30% more likely to intend to leave than their white counterparts.[4]

It doesn't have to be this way. The need for diversity, equity, and inclusion (DEI) may be obvious to some but not all. In some cases, you may have to "sell" the importance of DEI to the powers that be—whether that's your manager, HR team, or C-Suite executives.

Diversity is about differences and the number of people with differences. I'll explore this more in the next chapter, but diversity isn't valuable unless underrepresented people feel included. You'll notice that as a recurring theme throughout the book. As you look to make the case for DEI initiatives within your organization, and as you begin to implement these initiatives, don't just focus on diversity! You must also focus on equity and inclusion.

Here are some strong selling points to make the case for comprehensive DEI initiatives within your own organization:

You'll better understand the needs of your target client.

When a workforce is diverse, that talent has a broader understanding of the needs of their diverse clients. Naturally, when an organization better understands the needs of its target market, it can better innovate their products and services—and that leads to an increase in revenue.

According to their 2016 analysis of more than 20,000 global firms, McKinsey & Co. found that companies leading in executive board diversity had returns that were 53% higher than others. Organizations with high rates of female executives were also more profitable.

McKinsey & Co. also found that companies that exhibit gender and ethnic diversity are, respectively, 15% and 35% more likely to perform better than those that don't. Their research shows that organizations with more racial and gender diversity also have better sales revenue, more customers, and higher profits. [5]

You'll save money in employee turnover.

Not only can comprehensive DEI strategies lead to higher revenue, but they can also save companies money in employee turnover. Millennials, who most value diversity, make up 35% of the workforce. Generation Z is bigger still—and right behind them in valuing diversity. Leaders must pay attention to their needs. According to Deloitte's 2016 Millennial survey, 66% of the Millennials (including 57% of those in senior positions) expect to change jobs in the next five years. [6] And according to ZipRecruiter's survey of more than 6,000 job seekers, 86% of job seekers said that a diverse workforce is an important factor when evaluating companies and job offers. [7]

These employees want to work for companies and organizations where diversity and equality matter, and if they don't work in that type of environment, they're more likely to leave. That gets expensive. According to the Society of Human Resources Management, it costs six to nine months salary to replace an employee. You'll save money by investing in your employees.[8]

You'll create champions of your brand.

While diverse teams are important, a comprehensive diversity, equity, and inclusion strategy is necessary to truly reap financial benefits. Diversity is the people: the mix of everyone on the team. Equity is policies and systems that give underrepresented people a fair shot to succeed. Inclusion is the strategy of ensuring the diverse mix of people feel welcome, are given a voice, and have permission to truly be themselves at work.

Without comprehensive DEI strategies that include buy-in from leadership, diversity initiatives by themselves are ultimately shallow and employees will leave. Diversity and inclusion work has to be authentic to be effective; you can't just check boxes.

You may find yourself as the lone diversity, equity, and inclusion evangelist in your organization, but you cannot venture this journey alone. It's critical to build a coalition of people who share the same ideals, especially those who are also leaders or influencers of leaders. With authentic investment from leadership and a comprehensive DEI strategy, organizations will see benefits that go far beyond increased revenue.

According to Gallup, *"Companies with highly engaged workforces outperform their peers by 147% in earnings per share."* An engaged, included workforce means that employees can express their passions at work, allowing them to effectively be champions of projects that will ultimately advance the company's mission. Their passion leads them to be agents of positive change within the company.[9]

This work is hard, but the rewards are great. You now know some of the facts confirming why diversity contributes to the bottom line. Next, I'll show you HOW to implement a program that is genuine, authentic, and truly drives results.

Leverage the data

Most people want to be more accepting. They want to help but they need to find their own WHY. Once they have that, you can show them all of the "hows" in this book. Helping your team find their own WHYs and getting buy-in for your proposed DEI initiatives boils down to data and storytelling.

Unfortunately, as you may have noticed from watching the news, fear sells. Senior leaders may actually be more receptive to data about what can be *lost* by not having a diverse workforce who feels included, valued, and empowered, versus what can be gained by having a diverse workforce.

To help you make this case and get that buy-in with the leaders of your organization, I've compiled some statistics about the importance of a diverse workforce who feels included, valued, and empowered. There's clear data about the financial rewards.

It may also be compelling to consider the ramifications of customers and clients who have a negative experience with your brand because of the side effect of a lack of diversity. I'll share some of those numbers, too.

Let's get started.

In a McKinsey study, companies in the bottom quartile in terms of gender and ethnic diversity are 29% more likely to underperform the national average in profitability when compared to companies with more diversity.[10]

Coqual revealed that companies with diverse teams are 70% more likely to report the capture of a new market within the past year. Those same companies were almost 50% more likely to report market growth in the prior year.[11]

The 2020 Edelman Trust Barometer Special Report found that people were up to four and a half times more likely to say a brand would earn or keep their trust by acting in response to racial injustice.[12]

Sales teams with at least one member sharing the ethnicity of the client are 152% more likely to fully understand the needs of that client, according to Harvard Business Review.[13]

According to the Edelman Trust Barometer, 76% of Americans believe corporations should take the lead on social change, rather than waiting for government to impose change.[14]

Start-ups with at least one woman founder get 21% more venture capital backing in later funding rounds. This is further proof that greater diversity leads to greater innovation, which leads to greater financial results.[15]

According to a Bloomberg study, hedge funds led by women and people of color outperformed other hedge funds by a massive 72%. The analysis compared 908 funds led by white men and 35 managed by women and people of color.[16]

A survey from the business news website The Manifest found that 70% of job seekers value a company's commitment to diversity when evaluating potential employers.[17]

Glassdoor.com did a survey of 5,000 job-seekers in the U.S. and Europe and found that 70% would not apply to work for a company whose values did not align with their own. In fact, 59% (and 65% of those between 18 and 34 years old) found culture more important than salary. "Culture" includes diversity and inclusion and this data is one more way to get buy-in for DEI initiatives at your organization.[18]

According to a Deloitte survey, 75% of Millennials believe an organization is more innovative when it fosters a culture of diversity and inclusion, and these employees are thus more likely to leave if the company doesn't meet their standards of diversity. If you want strong talent, you need DEI.[19]

Harvard Business Review studied Glassdoor.com reviews and compared them to the American Consumer Satisfaction Index and discovered a strong correlation. Happy employees = happy customers, with companies like Southwest Airlines, Trader Joe's, Costco, and Hilton setting great examples of this.[20]

All this to say: whether it's about increasing profit, decreasing turnover, or making your organization more appealing to Generation Z, diversity, equity, and inclusion matters!

Use this data to make the case to your organization's senior leaders and other key stakeholders. Then share this data with managers and directors who may be resistant to change. A commitment to DEI from everyone is needed to build an organization made for the future.

Follow the ARC

In my conversations with clients, I've found that many well-meaning organizations and people want to do the right thing to create a more inclusive culture, but they often don't know where to start. As a result, they don't start at all. Many stay inactive due to overwhelm or fear of messing up. They're afraid of saying or doing the wrong thing—so they do nothing.

I believe that if we don't know what to do or don't know what to say in any given situation, the best option is to ask a question.

How do you do that? *Follow the ARC.*

The ARC Method® is a tool I developed for my consulting firm to quickly move organizations (and people!) from a problem-oriented mindset to a solutions-oriented mindset. In our strategy sessions, workshops, and coaching, we explain how to Follow the ARC in order to create an inclusive culture.

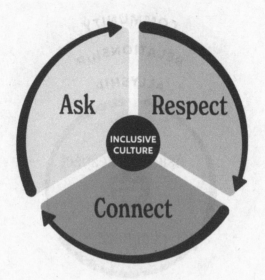

What's the ARC?

ARC is an acronym for ASK. RESPECT. CONNECT. The ARC Method* is a comprehensive set of concepts and tools that companies can use to build a more diverse and inclusive culture.

It does this by:

- Providing simple tools to apply DEI concepts in your day-to-day work.
- Showing people how to gain clarity around someone else's boundaries or differences.
- Offering insights and concepts that help shift people from problem to solution.
- Being flexible and robust enough to customize and apply to many different scenarios.

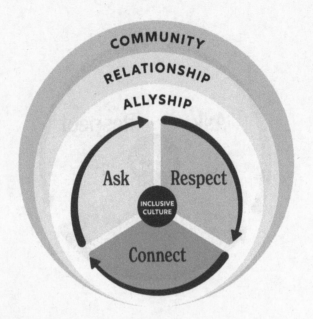

Applications

In what contexts do we Follow the ARC?

    1. A-llyship: Follow the ARC to become an ally if you witness something offensive.

    2. R-elationship: Follow the ARC to build authentic connections with others.

    3. C-ommunity: Follow the ARC to start or expand your organization's DEI goals.

Let's take a closer look at these various applications of the ARC Method® so you can see real-world examples of how to Follow the ARC.

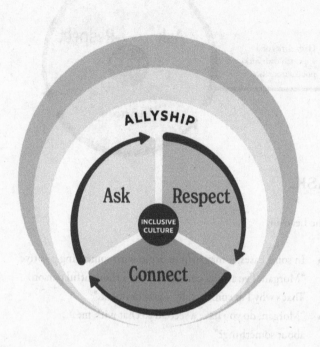

Application 1: Allyship

The first application is to follow the ARC to be a great ally. You becoming an ally is just as important as respecting people's differences. You can support others who may not be respected and gently call out comments that could be microaggressions or border on harassment. (A **microaggression** is defined as a subtle act of exclusion that marginalizes others. More on this later.)

Example: You're walking out of a meeting room and Morgan next to you leans over and mutters, "Ty is fitting in really well. I wasn't so sure since it's obvious the company is trying to increase diversity."

You feel uncomfortable and are not sure how to respond. You know a good ally doesn't let this go. Let's walk through this situation together using the ARC.

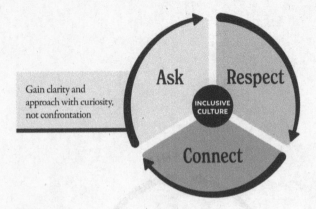

Gain clarity and approach with curiosity, not confrontation

ASK.

The Lead-in:

- In some cases, it may help to begin with something positive, "Morgan, I've always considered you a thoughtful person. That's why I'm confused by your comment."
- "Morgan, do you have a second to chat with me about something?"

The Question:

- "What did you mean by that comment about Ty being hired to increase diversity?"
- "Just so I'm clear, do you think Ty was hired just because of their race?"

Again, the ARC Method® helps people approach conversations from a place of curiosity, not confrontation, which reduces the risk of defensiveness from others.

Things to highlight in ASK:

- Make sure you approach someone privately at a time that works for both of you.
- When asking someone these questions, remember the goal is to seek information so you can have respectful dialogue—

even if there is a level of discomfort. You can choose to express how you feel if that helps break the tension.

- Avoid sarcasm when asking the question. Don't say something like: "What would YOU know about diversity?"

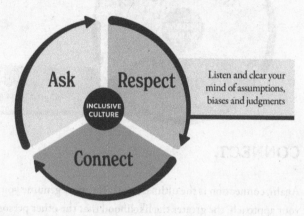

RESPECT.

Morgan may be caught off guard by your question but will still probably try to answer it. Morgan might say:

- "Oh, I was just joking! Ty is great."
- "I just mean that the company is always talking about diversity these days and Ty is the first person who's come along since we started having these conversations."
- "Yeah, I totally think Ty was hired because of their race. I mean, just look at this place. There's no one else like them."

Respecting Morgan means that you must actively listen. You don't dismiss the answer, and you don't interrupt.

Things to highlight in RESPECT:

- Even if you vehemently disagree, stay calm and focused on your end goal: to raise awareness that the comment was inappropriate.
- Put your phone down.
- Use positive, affirmative body language.

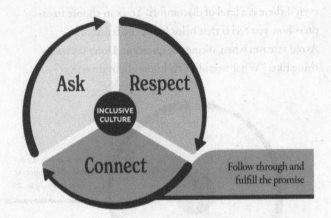

CONNECT.

Again, connection is the ultimate goal. The more genuine you are in your approach, the greater the likelihood that the other person will be more receptive, and the greater the opportunity to connect in an authentic way. People tend to be more open and accepting if they sense the other person has a positive intention.

Here are some examples with your coworker Morgan:

- "Ah, I couldn't tell that you were joking about Ty. Got it. FYI, I'm pretty sure Ty's been programming since they were seven-years-old and wasn't just hired to check a box."
- "OK, just so I'm clear, you don't really think Ty was a diversity hire? Cool, but just so you know, some people might be offended by that comment."
- "Got it. But when you say that it's actually offensive. Please don't say comments like that around me. Thanks!"

Things to highlight in CONNECT:

- Connecting can be brief. Connect and move on.
- Summarizing or paraphrasing the takeaways are two great ways to connect.
- Don't be afraid to be firm if the situation calls for it.

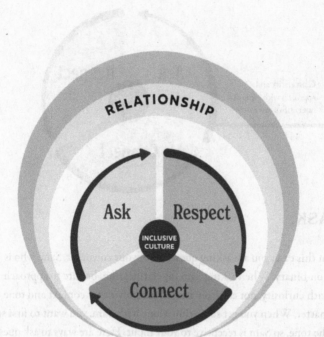

Application 2: Relationship

In this second application, an individual may feel unsure, confused, or uncomfortable about a one-on-one relationship that is new or unclear. The ARC Method® can be used to build clarity and a stronger, more authentic connection with others.

Example: a coworker has expressed themselves as **non-binary** and is using "they/them" **pronouns**, and you are not quite sure what that means. As a general rule, it is more effective to ask than assume, but what if you don't know how to ask? Let's walk through this situation together using the ARC.

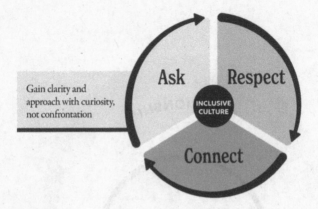

ASK.

In this case, you are asking questions of your coworker, Sam, who is non-binary. When asking Sam for clarification, be sure to approach with curiosity, not confrontation. Remember that context and tone matter. When you get some time alone with Sam, you want to first set the tone, so Sam is receptive to your input. Here are ways to ask questions in an open-minded, non-confrontational manner.

The Lead-in:

- "Sam, do you have a minute? I'd like to check in with you on something you said, and I want to make sure I'm saying the right thing."
- "Sam, I heard what you said about being non-binary. Can I ask you a quick question about that?"

The Question:

- "Can you tell me more about which pronouns I should be using?"
- "Exactly how would you like me to refer to you?"

The ARC Method* helps people approach conversations from a place of curiosity, not confrontation, which reduces the risk of defensiveness from others.

Things to highlight in ASK:

- Make sure you approach someone privately at a time that works for both of you.
- When asking someone these questions, remember the goal is to seek information so you can have respectful dialogue—even if there is a level of discomfort. You can choose to express how you feel if that helps break the tension.
- Notice the focus on behavior—not feelings.
  - o "I **heard**... You would like me to **say**...
    When I **refer to you**..."

Type of questions not to ask:

- A private personal question (i.e., do not ask: "When's the surgery?" to someone who is transgender).
- A question that can be answered by Google (i.e., do not ask: "What can I do to be antiracist?" to someone who is Black).

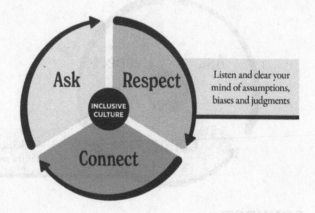

RESPECT.

Respect is where we clear our minds of assumptions, biases, and judgments which is extremely difficult because of the **unconscious bias**, also known as implicit bias, that we may have without realizing it.

(more on this in Chapter 2). It's being brave enough to stay open and honest with yourself and demonstrate your respect for others. This means that after you ask a question, you actively listen. You don't dismiss the answer, and you don't interrupt.

Sam could say a number of things, such as:

- "Thanks for asking. My pronouns are they/them."

Things to highlight in RESPECT:

- Use positive, affirmative body language.
- Put your phone down.
- Always affirm what you have heard and confirm their comfort level for moving forward.
- Articulate your behavior goal and ask for patience if needed.
- Commit to your behavior and mean it.

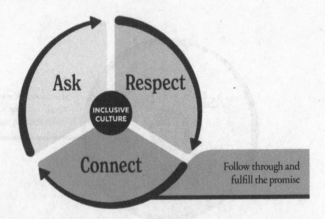

CONNECT.

This is the ultimate goal, to make that connection. To make something that becomes bigger than two people talking. It's about energy and expansion. Connection is about fulfilling the promise made by Asking and Respecting.

The more genuine you are, the more the person will feel comfortable, and the greater the opportunity to connect in an authentic way. People tend to be more open and accepting if they sense the other person has a positive intention.

Here are some examples with your coworker Sam:

- "Sam, to make sure I've got this right, you'd like me to refer to you as 'they/them' going forward when I'm referring to you?"
- "Then we agree? I commit to trying my best with this, and you'll try to be patient with me as I adjust to the pronouns."

Things to highlight in CONNECT:

- Connecting can be brief. Connect and move on.
- Summarizing or paraphrasing the takeaways are two great ways to connect.

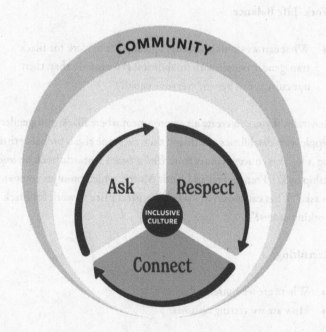

Application 3: Community

The third application is to follow the ARC on your organization's DEI journey. This approach can be used by a Diversity Council (more on this in Chapter 2), by people in Human Resources, or anyone taking the lead on DEI initiatives within the organization.

ASK.

Examples of ASK for systemic change:

Organizational Structure:

- What is the diversity makeup of our senior leadership team? Our board?
- What's our percentage of underrepresented talent in management roles?

Work/Life Balance:

- What can we do to make this a great place to work for Black transgender people with disabilities? If we can do that, then our culture can benefit everyone equally.

Generally, if you can create an environment where Black transgender people with disabilities can thrive, then everyone else is probably thriving, too. This concept comes from *Unleashed*, a fantastic book on leadership by Dr. Frances Frei and Anne Morris, which prompts companies to ask, "What can we do to make this a great place to work for Black working moms?" [21]

Recruiting:

- Where are we sourcing talent?
- How are we vetting résumés?

Client Service:

- How are we identifying and selecting our vendors?
- What sort of risk are we creating in the way we address our clients?

Job Advancement:

- How are stretch assignments offered?
- What's the performance review process?

Communication:

- What topics are we choosing to communicate internally?
- What audiences are we considering as we create materials and messaging?

RESPECT.

Respect is where we clear our minds of assumptions, biases, judgments—which is extremely difficult because of unconscious bias that is there without us realizing. It's being brave enough to stay open and honest with yourself and demonstrate your respect for others. This means that you actively listen, you don't dismiss the answer, and you don't interrupt. Often, this is the piece that many people feel is missing for them.

Here are more examples of how to respect:

- Respect the answers you may receive from employee inclusion surveys.
- Respect the data about the gender balance among managers.
- Respect the process for accountability for following through on changes.

CONNECT.

This is the ultimate goal—to make that connection something that is bigger than all of us. It's about energy and expansion, about fulfilling the promise made by Asking and Respecting.

- Connect the answer to solutions (you'll find many in this book!).
- Connect leaders' assessments to specific diversity and inclusion targets, or participation in DEI initiatives.
- Connect your employees to each other to hold open conversations, build more allies, and build more **sponsorship** relationships.

Follow all three applications of the ARC to become *Inclusive 360*.

Now, with the ARC Method® firmly in hand, off we go into the wonderful work of creating a more equitable world. The world needs you today.

You've got this.

Get the ARC Method® cheat sheet at
TheEqualityInstitute.com/arc

MANY WELL-MEANING ORGANIZATIONS and people want to do the right thing to create a more inclusive culture, but they often don't know where to start. As a result, they don't start at all. Many stay inactive due to overwhelm or fear of messing up. They're afraid of saying or doing the wrong thing—so they do nothing.

I believe that if we don't know what to do or don't know what to say in any given situation, the best option is to ask a question.

How do you do that? *Follow the ARC.*

CHAPTER 2

Born this Way
Understanding Diversity

Define diversity

WHAT IS DIVERSITY? I'll keep it simple: it's a mix, in this case, a mix of people. Diversity can include various identity elements such as race, gender, and sexual orientation. It can also include personality characteristics, learning styles, political leanings, and more. Some elements of diversity are visible while others are not.

Throughout this book, I'll be as specific as I can when I talk about different types of underrepresented people, but a term you'll see often is **BIPOC**. BIPOC means Black, Indigenous and People of Color. This term is slightly broader than "people of color," which you may currently use.

A little bit about me, in case you were wondering: my race is white. My gender is a cisgender woman. My sexual orientation is lesbian. I'm a first-generation American, an ENFJ, a DI, a Sagittarius, and a mom.

There are many dimensions to me, just like there are many dimensions to you. Those layers of identity stack on top of each other and they compound. The more **marginalized identities** someone has, the fewer advantages they generally have. This concept of intersecting identities is called **intersectionality** and was first coined by Kimberlé Williams Crenshaw in 1989, when she used it to describe how race, gender, and class can compound to create an entirely different and more challenging lived experience for people with multiple marginalized identities. [22]

This means that often a white gay woman like me has more advantages than a Black woman, especially a Black transgender woman. But I might not have as many advantages as a white gay man because women are generally more marginalized than men, even gay men (like with the gender pay gap, which is addressed in Chapter 5). That's not always the case, but it is often enough.

I believe that the more advantages you have, the more you should use those advantages to help others out and lift others up. We will discuss this more in the section on equity.

Ideally, organizations should be looking to increase diversity for the reasons I described in the first chapter. They are ideally looking to also promote and retain their underrepresented talent. Of course, that's easier said than done, but stick with me and I'll share successfully proven tactics in this section.

Understand unconscious bias

When was the last time you made an assumption about a person and guessed wrong? You probably do it all the time. I know I do.

I'll never forget the time I ran into a former client whom I hadn't seen in years. We exchanged hellos, and then I looked at her tummy and asked, "When's the baby due?"

She said something I'll never forget: "I had the baby three months ago."

I saw her tummy and made an assumption that she was pregnant. I guessed wrong, and it was really awkward.

It's certainly not the first time I've made assumptions and guessed wrong. I'm blessed with gaydar. You know, gay-radar. The superpower that us LGBTQ+ people have that allows us to detect others who are LGBTQ+.

Well, gaydar is based on assumptions and stereotypes, and guess what? I've guessed wrong plenty of times in the past. There are a few embarrassing stories I'll leave out of this book.

I'll never forget the time someone made an assumption about me. My partner, Heather, and I were on a walk with one of the kids. We walked by a house where a woman in the yard called out, "Oh, look at you sweet mother-daughter." She was clearly referring to Heather and her daughter.

Then the woman turned to me (with short hair and breasts) and said, "And you must be the dad!"

Ouch. I didn't like that one bit. Did our neighbor assume that I'm the "man" in my same-sex relationship?

I laughed it off, but it bothered me. I didn't like being put in a box. I didn't like that assumption.

At the end of the day, her assumption wasn't a big deal. We laughed off a little awkwardness and moved on. But some assumptions can cause real harm, and just like assumptions show up in real life, they also show up all the time at work.

There could be a deeper reason why people make assumptions. You can blame the amygdala. Did you know that our brains are overwhelmed with millions of stimuli every minute? Background sounds, peripheral images, and more saturate our brain. How can our brain possibly process that much data? For our brains, it's easy. Our brains have been well-trained to do this for centuries as sapiens have evolved from hunter-gatherers to today's modern humans.

The amygdala glands of the brain actually organize this data for easy recall—and to keep us safe. The amygdala organizes stimuli so rapidly by categorizing data with similar qualities into tiny little boxes in our brain. In the days of hunter-gatherers, data was organized and recalled quickly to direct those sapiens into "fight" or "flight"—run from the tiger or fight it! The amygdala is our body's primal instinct.

Centuries later, those fears are largely irrelevant, but the amygdala is still busy categorizing every bit of stimuli that comes our way—again, to keep us safe. For example, it categorizes objects such as "knives" as being sharp, and tells us to be careful. It categorizes "boiling water" as hot, and tells us to be careful. It simply, instinctively, categorizes things which are similar—but not just things, people as well.

New York University researchers discovered that the way the amygdala works is a major contributing factor to unconscious bias, also known as implicit bias.[23]

Unconscious bias is the act of instinctively making assumptions about people or things without taking the time to really understand a situation or think things through. We're all guilty of this. Every last one of us, including me.

Unconscious bias is just another form of an assumption. We all make assumptions because of the ways our brains have been wired for centuries to make decisions quickly to keep us safe. Unfortunately, unconscious bias leads to all sorts of problems. It prevents people from seeing the full picture or considering other alternatives. This can cause big problems at work.

To give you an example, Dr. Tamika Cross was flying on Delta Airlines back in 2016 when the flight attendant made an announcement that there was a medical emergency and asked if there was a doctor on board. Dr. Cross rang her call button and informed the flight attendant that she was a physician. *"Oh no sweetie put your hand down, we are looking for actual physicians or nurses or some type of medical personnel, we don't have time to talk to you,"* reported the flight attendant.

When Dr. Cross explained she was a physician, the flight attendant asked about credentials (which she didn't have when traveling for a wedding), but then accepted help from a white male physician who also did not show credentials.

Dr. Cross believed that the flight attendant dismissed her because she's a Black woman—and the flight attendant's unconscious bias might have told her, "Black women can't be doctors." In an emergency situation, the amygdala took over.

Dr. Cross shared the story on Facebook, and it went viral. There were 91,000 likes, 22,000 comments, and 48,000 shares—on Facebook alone. Delta paid attention, brought Dr. Cross in for a meeting, apologized, and changed its policy to never require credentials before assisting passengers experiencing a medical emergency. [24]

Delta's not the only major organization whose frontline team ended up in hot water because of unconscious bias. You may have heard about the employee at a Starbucks in Philadelphia who called the police on two Black men who were sitting in the restaurant waiting for a friend. They had not yet ordered. The police arrested the men on trespassing charges, just as their friend was arriving. The scene was captured on video and went viral.

Starbucks was in hot water from this incident and responded strongly, closing all corporate stores for a half-day to provide unconscious bias training for all employees. The company now also includes unconscious bias training as part of their new hire training program. While training doesn't solve all problems, it's a step in the right direction. According to analysts at Bloomberg Financial, this incident cost Starbucks at least $16.7 million in lost sales alone. [25]

Those stories went viral—and for good reason. It's great that there were actions taken after each of the incidents, but unconscious bias happens to each of us, a thousand times a day—and it happens in the workplace all of the time.

Unconscious bias leads to a lack of diversity in hiring and promotions, where people with privilege and power unconsciously tend to hire and promote others like them. Again, our brain wants us to choose the safe and familiar choice, perhaps the choice most similar to ourselves.

These beautiful people are not my real network, but chosen as avatars of them. [26]

I know what this is like. I love all of the people in this photo. They are some of my closest friends and colleagues and, as of about six years ago, they were my tightest network. If I had opportunities to give, if I had stretch assignments, or if I had referrals to give, I would have given them to these people.

Most of these people are women. Most of them are lesbians, or somehow part of the LGBTQ+ community. Most of them are white. Most of them are parents. And most of them are right around my age.

In other words, these are people just like me!

So why did I do this? It's not like I was intentionally trying to exclude other people. Drawing people like me towards me, letting those people be closer, is my brain's way of keeping me safe and comfortable. It's a subconscious assumption, a shortcut, that guides me to believe people who are like me are safe.

I still love those people. They're amazing, but my network is much more diverse now. I took the time to get to know people who are different from me, to invite people of color and transgender folks out to coffee or out to a drink after an event, or for a virtual meetup. I became intentional about starting conversations with people who are different from me.

When you don't set the intention and take the time to be deliberate about including others (to create more diversity), you default to excluding others. Inclusion requires intention. And often, unconscious bias leads to homogeneity within organizations. The people in charge often unconsciously surround themselves with others like them—again, because they're safe and familiar.

This plays out in organizations everywhere, and you can see it visually represented on the "Meet the Team" web page of many organizations, where leadership teams are often overwhelmingly white and male.

Here are some of the ways unconscious bias shows up in human resources:

Gender bias: women are given fewer opportunities than men if they have kids but are disliked when they are not seen as nurturing.

Association bias: favoring those who went to the same college, are members of the same organization or association, are from your home state, etc.

Similarity bias: hiring/promoting someone that is similar to the person who previously had the position, similar to others in the department, and/or similar to the interviewer.

Ultimately, if you are a hiring manager and your unconscious bias leads you to hire someone who is in your own demographic and from your home state, you are making an assumption about their ability to perform in a way that is similar to you. You are unconsciously assuming that because they are like you, that they are as talented and easy to work with as you are, and that they will fit right in at the organization.

It feels bad to think that our unconscious mind causes us to have bias towards others or have bias that excludes others, but it does. That's why unconscious bias training is a foundational piece of any diversity, equity, and inclusion program.

I challenge you to reflect: how diverse is your network? Does your network primarily look like you? Does your network primarily check the same or similar demographic boxes as you? And if so, how can you be a little bit more deliberate about including folks who are different from you?

I'll admit that it took a bit of courage to ask people out for networking dates. There was a bit of fear of rejection. On a few occasions, I was even afraid people thought I was hitting on them!

But I asked anyway and made some great new friends.

My network is a lot more diverse now. I now can offer opportunities and referrals to wonderful Black and brown people and to brilliant transgender people.

And even to some straight white men.

Before undertaking specific DEI initiatives, I'd highly encourage you to explore the foundational topic of unconscious bias. Establishing a common language and common goals around unconscious bias and diversity will go a long way towards ensuring the success of whatever initiatives you choose. I'll share more on unconscious bias training in Chapter 10.

Establish your baseline

As the saying goes, what gets measured, gets managed. It's hard to know where to go if you're not completely clear where you are. It's time to start looking at your organization's own data so you can set some clear, measurable goals for the future.

I wrote about the basics of the ARC Method* in the previous chapter, but now we'll dig in. The ARC Method* is a tool I use with organizations to quickly become solutions-oriented.

Remember, you might not like what you find when you ask the following questions. You might find that you have an awful lot of work to do. But it's critical to know where you're starting from.

ASK.

Ask the hard questions. Ask the questions everyone is afraid to know the answer to. Ask about tradeoffs. Ask about the data. Ask your people.

Ask questions such as:

- How many women are in Director level or higher roles? How many BIPOC?
- What is the diversity makeup of our leadership team? Our Board?
- What is the turnover rate of BIPOC employees vs white employees?
- Which departments have the highest percentages of BIPOC employees?
- Which departments have the highest percentages of women?

RESPECT.

Respect the answers you find when you ask questions like those above. Actively listen to the numbers and the data—even if you don't like what it tells you. Especially if you don't like what it tells you. Don't dismiss what you find.

Thoughtfully listen to those who are brave enough to share their stories and respect their stories. Respect the process for change.

CONNECT.

Connect these answers to solutions. Connect solutions to accountability systems. And connect the accountability for solutions to leaders' assessments, so leaders are more invested in the change. Using the ARC Method®, you are moving from a problem to a solution. You can use the ARC Method® to guide your organization towards increasing diversity.

Let's open up your Human Resources Information System (HRIS) and get started. You may already have much of this information available in your HRIS from affirmative action plans and Equal Employment Opportunity reporting obligations. That might not cover it all. More likely, you'll need to survey your workforce through voluntary self-identification to collect data such as religious affiliation and sexual orientation.

Here's the data I'd suggest you start collecting and analyzing [27]:

- Percentages of employees by race and gender
- Turnover rate by race and gender
- Percentage of new hires in each department by race and gender
- Gender, birth date, parental status, race, veteran status, and disability status—sorted by tenure and department
- Hires by month by team
- Hires by month by race
- Hires by tenure

Make no mistake: it may be challenging to gather diversity data from employees initially, especially when employees are unsure of how the data will be used or if there is general distrust of leadership in an organization. If this is the case, an organization may want to use a third party or survey technology to capture information that will be reported in aggregate without identifying information.

Take this data and notice the trends. What do you see? You might find that your organization is pretty typical. This is often what we find when my firm conducts Human Resources audits:

- BIPOC are disproportionally in lower-level positions and in Operations and Human Resources.
- Women are disproportionally in Human Resources and Marketing.
- Men and Asian people are heavily weighted in technology.
- Senior leadership are primarily straight, white, cisgender, men.

If you're seeing similar trends within your own organization, that's OK. We're just getting started. And now you've established a baseline.

Set diversity targets

Now that you've started to figure out where you are, you can start to think about where you want to go as an organization. Just how diverse do you want to be?

Ed Bastian, CEO of Delta, shares, *"It's not quotas. It's about raising the bar for everybody. We need to give people the benefit of the doubt. Not the presumption that they can't, and giving them that opportunity, and realizing people don't come from traditional backgrounds."* [28]

Your organization is not going to magically become more diverse overnight. Because of unconscious bias, building a diverse workforce doesn't happen by accident. It must be done with intention. In fact, research from The Institute for Gender and the Economy (GATE) shows that a "shock to the system" is necessary because of how ingrained our unconscious biases are.

It helps to set some diversity targets. Some might call them quotas, but I'll stick with diversity targets, for clarity's sake. These can be set in order to increase the number of women, people of color, veterans, or any other underrepresented group.

In 2020, many major companies announced workforce diversity targets.

- Wells Fargo & Co., the nation's third-biggest bank, said it will increase Black leadership to 12% over the next five years.
- Ralph Lauren Corp. said it aims to make 20% of its global leaders people of color by 2023.
- Delta Air Lines Inc., where 7% of the top 100 in the organization are Black, committed to doubling the percentage of Black officers and directors by 2025.
- Target committed to increase representation of Black team members across the company by 20% over the next three years. [29]

Additionally, in 2020, 27 firms (including Amazon and JP Morgan Chase) formed the NY Jobs CEO Council. Their commitment is to hire 100,000 people from low-income Black, Latino, and Asian communities by 2030.[30]

Still, there's a lot of hesitation and hostility regarding diversity targets. You may hear comments like, "So, are we just going to stop hiring white men now?"

You may hear rumblings from others, "Oh, she was only hired because of the quota. We're lowering the bar."

But would your organization be lowering the bar? Do you honestly believe your organization would intentionally set itself up to fail by hiring a less-qualified candidate? Absolutely not.

Even the new hire may feel stigmatized and think to themself, "Was I hired because of the quota, or because I'm awesome?"

Perception is always different from reality.

GATE research shows that few underrepresented people who have been hired because of a diversity target report feeling stigmatized or isolated. And once there are enough of them, hopefully they will no longer be marginalized.[31]

Research shows that diversity targets lead talent acquisition teams to be more creative in their search for candidates, wildly expanding the talent pool.

If your organization decides to set some diversity targets, here are some best practices in effectively establishing and communicating this initiative:

- Get full commitment from leadership: your senior leaders must buy-in to this initiative and agree to set specific targets.

- The targets should be a standing agenda item on Human Resources talent acquisition team meetings so there's a team commitment to achieving it.
- Leaders should be held accountable for their achievement of these targets in their own performance metrics.
- Proactively mitigate any negative effects (such as imposter syndrome) this could have on underrepresented candidates joining the team while the targets are set. Ensure that managers reinforce with new hires why they were hired, and why they're so excited that the candidate chose to join the organization. Work with the new hires to create professional development plans so they see a career path forward within the organization.

Makes sense, right? Of course, it's not always easy—at least the first time. But we'll continue to discuss ways to expand the talent pool in the next chapter.

Establish a diversity council

Even if you don't have the budget for a full-time DEI employee, a key step is to start a DEI Council or committee.

The goal here is to enlist leaders who will use their seniority to advocate for DEI initiatives. Involve 10–30 volunteer leaders from all parts of the organization, especially those with a large span of responsibility. Effective councils include department heads and other line executives, as well as members of underrepresented groups.

Members should be tasked to further educate themselves (give them this book!), then drive and inform DEI strategy and initiatives. Councils can analyze information on diversity for the whole organization, for business units, and for departments to figure out what needs attention and then develop strategic action plans for change. Council members should not be expected to be subject matter experts or stand-ins for a paid DEI team.

DEI Council members should be people who are already convinced of the value of a diverse, equitable, and inclusive organization, even if they're not clear on the path forward. Try to identify people you know are already clear on their "why," because members will be asked to advocate to the "resisters," or those who do not see the value of DEI, at the organization.

When my team is working with an organization, we often work closely with the DEI Council. Some members serve as a focus group for us and share their individual perspectives on their experience with and visions for the organization. We typically deliver our findings to the DEI Council first, then work with them on implementing policy changes and launching initiatives. The Council is the hub, especially for smaller organizations without paid DEI staff.

A key first activity for the DEI Council is establishing a DEI strategic plan for your organization. This is ideally a five-year plan full of suggested policy changes and initiatives that will advance DEI. Some are short-term wins and others are long-term projects.

In order to create a DEI strategic plan, you'll need to assess the organization's current state. For us, this means conducting interviews, leading focus groups, looking closely at existing hiring and promotion policies and employee benefits, conducting an employee survey, and much more. You can use the ARC questions from this chapter to explore internally, or hire an outside firm to conduct a formal assessment of your organization.

In examining your organization's policies, you'll start to see some obvious diversity and inclusion gaps (and some less obvious ones) that should be addressed in the strategic plan. Key themes will emerge, and you'll be able to identify the low-hanging fruit of policy changes and initiatives that can provide quick wins for the DEI Council to share widely and build momentum.

Your DEI Council should not just focus on those low-hanging fruit projects, like planning Women's History Month programming. To truly make a difference, ensure that the Council also takes on initiatives that address creating more equitable systems. This book is full of ideas that can inform your organization's DEI strategy.

This book offers many solutions, and Council members can each read it and highlight what they would consider to be quick wins for which they can get easy approval. The Council can then collaborate and discuss ideas from this book that make sense as long-term initiatives, then create groups to focus on specific themes (such as hiring, promotions, etc.).

Inclusive 360 Action Steps

- ☐ Use the ARC Method* to identify baseline diversity data for your organization.
- ☐ Compile a list of key trends in your baseline data.
- ☐ Establish specific diversity targets and systems of accountability for those targets.
- ☐ Establish a cross-functional DEI Council/Committee/Task Force for your organization.

Keep learning:

- Book: Authentic Diversity by Michelle Silverthorn
- Book: Thinking, Fast and Slow by Daniel Kahneman
- Book: Blindspot by Mahzarin R. Banaji

WHEN WE DON'T set the intention and take the time to be deliberate about including others (to create more diversity), we default to excluding others. Inclusion requires intention. How can you be more deliberate about including folks who are different from you?

Formation
Increasing
Diversity

Understand the broken pipeline

YOU MAY HAVE heard the story of a man named Jose, who was having no luck with his job applications. He began applying with the name "Joe" instead, and suddenly started receiving calls. The same is true in numerous studies where two résumés were submitted for the same job that were identical in all aspects except for one: the name. People who have white, male sounding names like John and Bob are more likely to get call backs. Additionally, résumés with male names consistently get more calls for interviews than identical résumés with female names.[32]

Underrepresented folks often don't get jobs due to bias in the talent acquisition process. The process is riddled with hidden, unconscious bias, and because it's unconscious, the best solutions are systemic ones.

Here I'll address some of the solutions that can be used within the talent acquisition process. It takes intention to recruit underrepresented folks and to ensure your hiring process gives them a fair shot.

Analyze your talent acquisition process by taking it through the ARC Method®.

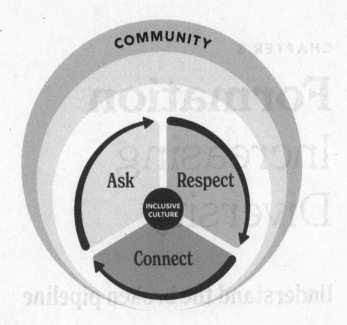

ASK.

Start by asking questions such as:

- Where do we source our talent? Are there any sources that generally lead to more candidates from underrepresented groups?
- How often do these candidates move to the next step? What's the percentage compared to white candidates? What about compared to white male candidates?
- Why are these candidates rejected? At what stage are they rejected? Are there particular leaders who reject these candidates disproportionally?
- Do you have clear hiring criteria with standardized questions and hiring committees for each candidate? Or is hiring criteria variable and fluid?
- Do you collect written feedback about candidates?

- Do underrepresented candidates have different experiences (such as extra interviews or background checks) than other candidates?

Some of these questions are ones you can easily look up. The harder questions may involve actually interviewing new hires and asking them about their experience. Other questions may involve conversations with hiring managers to reflect on their experiences. The process is both quantitative and qualitative.

RESPECT.

Respect the answers. Actively look at the numbers and the data. Don't dismiss the stories you hear and the numbers you find. Thoughtfully listen to the experiences of candidates and recruiters and respect their stories. Respect the process for change.

CONNECT.

Again, connect these answers to solutions like some of those in this book. Connect solutions to accountability systems. And connect the accountability for solutions to leaders' assessments. Connect your employees to each other to hold open conversations.

You can use the ARC Method® to guide your organization towards increased diversity.

Follow the ARC. Ask. Respect. Connect. Move from problem to solution. Solutions like:

Expand the pipeline

One of the main excuses organizations use when explaining a lack of gender diversity is a pipeline issue. They may say that they're simply not receiving many job applications from qualified underrepresented talent.

In the 2018 Preqin Investor Survey, Sandra Legrand from Alter Domus, a private equity firm, shared, *"Diversity begins at the lower levels, starting with private equity education programs in universities to build up a pipeline of talent. Stirring up the curiosity of young women by sharing knowledge and experience, as well as participating in coaching and mentoring programs, will lead to increased diversity within our industry."* [33]

It can and should absolutely include stirring the curiosity of young talent by reaching into universities to provide coaching, mentorships, and internships, but there are some quicker ways you can get started.

1. Ditch the résumés.

The investment firm Capital Group decided to no longer show résumés of internship candidates to hiring managers. Instead, managers focused more on the same set of questions about work ethic, background, and experience. Candidates were given a video to let them know the hiring manager hasn't seen the résumés and to otherwise prepare them for the interview process. The result was 50/50 gender balance and 58% people of color among the internship class. [34]

2. Use empathetic language.

HubSpot uses empowering and empathetic language in its job postings. It reads, in part: *"However you identify and whatever background you bring with you, please apply if this is a role that would make you excited to come into work every day."* [35]

This sends a clear signal to people with marginalized identities that they are welcome.

3. Weed out biased words in job descriptions.

Job descriptions often have hidden biases that attract male candidates over women. For example, driven, competitive, and analyze are male-bi-

ased words while collaborate, loyal, and support are words that are fe-
male-biased.

There's actually a solution to the unconscious biases that show up in
job descriptions: Textio software notices biases when someone is typing a job description and suggests more neutral changes. This simple
change will begin to attract a more balanced talent pool.

4. Incentivize your underrepresented talent's help.

As you learned in Chapter 2, unconscious bias generally causes us to
stick together with others like us. This can be an advantage when looking to source more underrepresented talent. Pinterest asks its employees who are not on the talent acquisition team for "loose referrals" or
"leads" and lets the recruiting team decide whether a particular candidate moves forward.[36]

Back in 2015, Intel doubled the referral bonus to get more wom-
en and other underrepresented people in the company and now pay
$4,000 for qualified referrals. According to a spokesperson, *"This is not
the first time we have offered employees referral incentives for diverse candidates, and it's a commonly used recruitment tool for businesses. Today,
it's one of many programs we are deploying to attract talented women and
underrepresented minorities to Intel."* [37]

5. Re-Consider degree requirements.

Consider whether specific degree requirements are necessary to work
in a job role. For example, you may find that a former biochemistry
major understands thermodynamics and therefore better understands
non-linear systems similar to equity markets. Social science majors who
understand cultural differences may be perfect for client-facing roles.
Your best candidates may bring nontraditional degrees or experiences.

I had a conversation recently with the COO of a hedge fund who
complained to me: *I just don't know where to look for a Black person with
a PhD in statistics.*

I told him that he was asking the wrong question. The question should not be, "Where do I find a Black person with a PhD in statistics?" but "Why do we require a PhD in statistics?" This is an important change in perspective, particularly given that the hiring process has blind assessments built in.

In fact, at IBM, a company with 350,000 global employees, 43% of open positions no longer require a college degree.[38] Google has taken a similar approach and now offers affordable six-month educational certificate programs in project management and data analysis. Google is treating these certificates as equal to a four-year college degree.[39]

These policy changes reduce the barriers to well-paying jobs for underrepresented talent.

6. Work from Anywhere (WFA).

The COVID-19 pandemic taught us that people could successfully work from home and stay productive. Many people took the opportunity to move away (at least temporarily) from high-priced cities such as San Francisco and New York, places that might not be ideal locations to ride out a pandemic. Others started their jobs remotely and still have never set foot in the office. When employees aren't forced to come into the office every day, they have more flexibility in where they live and may choose to live in more cost-effective cities and towns.

Work from Anywhere (WFA) policies can expand the talent pool by removing location as a hiring criteria. Due to systemic racism, homophobia, and so on, people from marginalized groups may struggle to afford the cost of living in major tech hubs such as the Bay Area of California. As an example, only 5% of San Francisco's residents are Black compared to 13.4% of the U.S. population. Research shows that for entry-level roles, Black candidates are highly unlikely to relocate for a position, especially if there is no relocation stipend provided.[40]

When allowing WFA policies, organizations can recruit diverse talent from just about anywhere in the world. Recruiters are able to cast a wider net and reach significantly more candidates who might prefer not to live in high cost, high-energy cities like New York City or San Francisco. Employees can choose where they live based on cost-of-living preferences and environments that feel right to them. This leads to more fulfilled employees.

According to the Centers for Disease Control and Prevention, one in four U.S. adults, or 61 million Americans, live with a disability that impacts major life activities. People with a mobility disability (one in seven U.S. adults) often experience difficulties with commutes, workplace **accessibility**, and stigmas regarding their work performance. Remote work can not only help eliminate workplace friction for people with disabilities, but also make it possible for employers to tap into a large group of workers with disabilities who are not currently in the labor force.[41]

By working remotely, those with disabilities can work in their own environment already tailored to their needs. Remote work may also allow people with disabilities to develop relationships in a setting where their disability is less obvious.

Beyond the cost-of-living issue, many people from underrepresented populations prefer remote work to minimize microaggressions (more on this in Chapter 14) or to have the flexibility to better care for loved ones.

Flexible, remote work can also be attractive to working parents and other caregivers who, amid the ongoing COVID-19 pandemic, have faced increased demands and reverted to more traditional household gender roles.

"Remote work allows women to work from wherever they feel most productive and watch their children grow up without having to hit pause on their career progression," Andrea Loubier, CEO of Mailbird, wrote in a Forbes article. *"And for women who are not mothers, this policy is still attractive. It gives them peace of mind that they do not have to put their*

career goals on the back burner, and it gives them all the other benefits of remote work in the meantime." [42]

Abstract, a tech company, has employees in 30 U.S. states and has a remote-first approach specifically to give their employees the choice to live somewhere they feel they belong. Underrepresented employees may find that sense of community and belonging outside of the major tech hub cities. [43]

"I've been learning from many of our underrepresented employees that starting over in a new community can feel jarring, isolating, and even unsafe," Kevin Smith, Abstract's cofounder, explains on the company's blog. *"They've shared that it's because, for some underrepresented people, communities often serve as a place for protection, support, and advocacy... When seen through this lens, asking people to choose between their livelihood and their community weakens the individual and the community from which they are being separated."* [44]

Spotify, Salesforce, and Dropbox are among the larger companies that announced a WFA policy, and Spotify specifically mentioned that they see it as one way to expand their talent pool. [45]

7. Recruit differently.

A diverse talent pool is more accessible when you expand the recruitment process beyond the obvious fields and experiences. You may find candidates who might not have considered a career in an industry because no one in their family or circle of friends is employed in that same industry or has a degree in that field.

For your own organization, consider whether specific technical training is a prerequisite to success. Many industries require skills that can be obtained from a wide variety of majors and disciplines. Let's take a look at some candidates you may not have previously proactively considered.

Consider veterans.

Forty-six percent of human resource professionals surveyed by the Society for Human Resource Management (SHRM) cited posttraumatic stress disorder (PTSD) and mental health issues as major challenges and barriers in considering employees with military experience, but veterans often bring valuable leadership and team experience.[46]

Bank of America and Hilton both achieved milestones when they exceeded their goals to hire more veterans. Bank of America exceeded its hiring goal of hiring 10,000 veterans in the past five years[47]; and Hilton has hired 30,000 in the past six years, with a goal to hire another 25,000 in the next five years.[48]

Consider refugees.

The CEO of Chobani Yogurt, Hamdi Ulukaya, a Turkish immigrant to the United States, is a big proponent of hiring refugees, which fast-tracks their integration into new communities. At Chobani's New York plant, 30% of the employees are immigrants and refugees, and more than 20 languages are spoken.[49]

Ulukaya is passionate about helping other organizations do the same. *"If you want to build a company that truly welcomes people-including refugees, one thing you have to do is throw out this notion of cheap labor. That's really awful. They're not a different group of people, they're not Africans or Asians or Nepalis. They're each just another team member. Let people be themselves, and if you have a cultural environment that welcomes everyone for who they are, it just works."*

Ulukaya created the non-profit organization, The Tent Partnership for Refugees, to help partner organizations hire refugees. Partners include Starbucks, IKEA, and Barilla. The Tent Partnership provides specific guidebooks on hiring and retaining refugees. In turn, many of the refugees that have been hired through The Tent Partnership have a low turnover rate.[50]

Consider people with autism.

About 85% of people who have Autism Spectrum Disorder (ASD) don't have gainful employment, even though some might have specialized skills that are in high demand—especially in the fields of science, technology, engineering, and math. More and more organizations are recognizing the unique value that **neurodiverse** talent can bring.[51]

Procter and Gamble (P&G) partnered on their neurodiverse hiring efforts with Specialisterne USA, a nonprofit that helps recruit and hire work-ready neurodiverse talent. The initial effort launched in February 2019 in Costa Rica and resulted in the hiring of six people with autism who work with a team in charge of providing software solutions and smart automation. Later that year, they hired four autistic managers at their new Cincinnati Neurodiversity Smart Automation Center. The company has already hired scientists, software engineers, and product researchers on the spectrum.[52]

In 2019, Dell Technologies launched a pilot Autism Hiring Program that included a two-week skills assessment for intern selection, followed by a 12-week summer internship for the selected adults with ASD. Since, several interns were hired as full-time employees. The program has now been expanded to Dell Technologies headquarters in Texas.

"We've seen tremendous talent come in through this program—talent that would otherwise be overlooked if we were not actively recruiting in these non-traditional ways," says Lou Candiello, Senior Manager of Diversity Talent Acquisition at Dell Technologies. *"We have filled critical positions across cybersecurity, data analytics, software engineering, artificial intelligence, and more with truly gifted and neurodiverse talent."*

To prepare for the initiative, Dell partnered with Horace Mann Educational Associates and local Arc affiliates to remove barriers that may limit a candidate from showing their true abilities and potential during an interview.[53]

Ultranauts also found great success hiring candidates on the autism spectrum. Seventy-five percent of employees are on the spectrum and work at all levels of the organization, including in leadership roles. Co-Founder Rajesh Anandan had witnessed people on the autism spectrum overlooked or struggling to fit in in the workplace.

"We started our company with the intention that neurodiversity, including autism, could be a competitive advantage for business. We fundamentally believe if we're able to bring together different brain types, different thinking styles, different processing models onto the same team and focused on the same work, we can do better, we can solve more complex problems." [54]

Consider people with criminal records.

Inequities in the criminal justice system and inequitable sentencing policies have negatively impacted Black and brown people, in particular, many of whom were jailed for minor offenses during the war on drugs. Many of these folks are now under-employed because employers often ask about an applicant's criminal history on the application.

According to JP Morgan Chase, the United States loses between $78 billion and $87 billion in annual Gross Domestic Product by excluding people who have a criminal record from the workforce. In late 2019, the unemployment rate for formerly incarcerated people was an estimated 27%, compared with 3.5% for the United States as a whole, according to the Prison Policy Initiative.

JP Morgan Chase removed the box on its applications that asks prospective employees whether they have a criminal record. The company has already hired 2,100+ people with a conviction on their record for entry-level jobs in software technology, lending, and account servicing. Crimes ranged from disorderly conduct to personal drug possessions and DUI charges. These low-level offenses often disqualify people from well-paying jobs. [55]

According to the National Employment Law Project, 35 states and more than 150 cities and counties have so-called "ban the box" laws that restrict criminal history questions on job applications. Hiring by financial institutions is regulated by the Federal Deposit Insurance Corporation, though in 2018, the agency began relaxing its rules, and JP Morgan Chase changed policies accordingly.

As it's expanding its pilot program in Chicago, JP Morgan is now partnering with organizations that specialize in training formerly incarcerated individuals, including Skills for Chicagoland's Future, Cara, The Safer Foundation and Cabrini Green Legal Aid.

Consider everyone.

The Body Shop has an "open hiring policy" for retail workers. It's remarkable: the first person who applies for the job gets it (as long as they can work in the U.S., stand for eight hours, and lift 50 pounds). There are no background checks and no drug tests. The jobs are available on a first come, first served basis.[56]

The Body Shop tested this at a distribution center and saw turnover decrease by 60%. They went from using three staffing agencies to only one. The money saved in recruiting, screening résumés, interviews, and background checks is redirected into training, employee benefits, and programs to support new employees with challenges such as transportation issues that can make it difficult for employees to get to work on time.

Andrea Blieden, the general manager of The Body Shop for the U.S., was told by supervisors who heard from employees, *"I've been struggling to find a job. This is one of the only places that would hire me, and I'm not going to mess this up."*

The Body Shop learned about this from Greyston Bakery, which pioneered this approach to build a company with $22 million in 2019 revenue. Greyston Bakery now runs a non-profit organization, The Greyston Center for Open Hiring, to help other organizations implement this process.[57]

Deep Dive:

PARTNERSHIP POSSIBILITIES

Partnerships are key. Here are some organizations that can help you fill your pipeline with diverse talent:

Veteran Talent

Wounded Warrior Project

Hiring Our Heroes

Workforce Opportunity Services

LGBTQ+ Talent

Lesbians Who Tech

Reach Out MBA (ROMBA)

TransCanWork

Out & Equal

Latinx Talent

Hispanic Alliance for Career Enhancement

National Hispanic Business Group

Association of Latino Professionals in Finance and Accounting

Prospanica

Society of Hispanic Human Resource Professionals

Black Talent

National Association of Black Accountants, Inc.

National Society of Black Engineers

National Association of African Americans in Human Resources

National Black Contractors Association

Executive Leadership Council

Asian Talent

National Association of Asian American Professionals

Society of Asian Scientists and Engineers

Ascend

Female Talent

National Association for Female Executives

Kayo Conference Series

Center for Women Executives

Network of Executive Women

Now that I've eliminated all excuses for you to blame the pipeline for a lack of diversity within your organization, it's time to explore what happens next. You have more underrepresented talent in your pipeline. Let's make sure they are set up for success as they move through the rest of the hiring process.

Fix the rest of the hiring process

As I've mentioned before, the hiring process is riddled with unconscious bias. We are especially drawn to familiarity, comfort, and simplicity. To minimize the unconscious bias in the hiring process, consider the following:

1. Be transparent about your hiring process.

Automattic, a software company, has a remarkably transparent and inclusive hiring process that acknowledges the unconscious biases that often come up in hiring. It's worth reading through Automattic's hiring page here: https://automattic.com/work-with-us/how-we-hire-developers/.

They share part of how they mitigate bias:

- *Training—we've found Facebook's course on Managing Bias and Google's workshop on Unconscious Bias @ Work to be quite effective.*
- *Using a standardized hiring rubric to ensure objectivity, fairness, and consistency.*
- *Documenting our hiring decisions with written evidence structured around the specific qualities we're looking for.*

And how they hire, including:

- Interview—a text-only interview conducted via a Slack chat to mirror the work experience at the company (and reduce any bias around appearance, verbal communication, and/or body language).

- Coding Challenge—a take home assessment.
- Work Trial—paid projects that will take about 40 hours to complete and allow both the company and the candidate to evaluate each other.

By communicating so clearly with candidates, Automattic reduces bias and expands the candidate pool.

2. Remove identifying data from résumés.

Software, such as Ideal, strips all identifying details (including name, location, and affiliations) from résumés so decisions on who to bring in for interviews are less biased. This allows interviewers to seek out candidates based on their qualifications, not based on any biases.

3. Give a work sample test.

It's common for tech companies to require work sample tests. But work samples don't have to be just for tech jobs. WeSolv is an online platform which connects underrepresented MBAs with organizations by creating online practical "challenges" that job seekers can anonymously solve. Employers can then choose candidates based on practical experience and fit—not based on the hidden biases they may bring to the hiring process. WeSolv and other work sample platforms allow performance to be a direct factor in hiring.

4. Have collaborative interviews with standardized questions.

Collaborative hiring with employees from diverse backgrounds reduces bias because more voices are part of the process. For those interviews, use standardized, role-based interview questions, which are important for many reasons: they force interviewers to focus on the factors that affect job performance; and if a scorecard with a one to five (or similar) scale is used as part of the process, this data can inform future hiring.

In 2021, SurveyMonkey, in partnership with Living Corporate, reported that in their study of 2,600 U.S. adults, 79% of job seekers today say it is important that they work for a place that hires people from diverse backgrounds. However, only one-third (34%) of people said they meet with a diverse panel of interviewers (every time or most of the time). That needs to change.[58]

5. Ask all candidates about their experiences with diversity, equity, and inclusion.

Diversity shouldn't just be something that matters to those from marginalized groups. All candidates can be asked questions that gauge their comfort level with, and experience with, DEI issues. These questions can help you bring on new talent who value DEI as much as your organization does. These questions can also show you which talent does not consider DEI important at all. Try these:

- Tell me about your experience working with diverse teams.
- How have you contributed to an inclusive workplace culture or community?
- Have you had the opportunity to act as someone's ally at work?

6. Normalize acceptance of parenthood and children.

Your employees need balance. Stripe, the payments processor, sends out an on-site interview guide to candidates that describes accommodations for nursing parents who interview in person. Since interviews often take all day, nursing parents may take short breaks and have access to a room for pumping.[59]

A lack of a diversity is a fixable problem.

Ask better questions to establish your baseline diversity data, respect the answers you find, then connect to some of the meaningful solutions in this chapter.

Deep Dive:

SOFTWARE TO REDUCE HIRING BIAS

There are many kinds of software solutions that can reduce bias within every aspect of your hiring process. These solutions use artificial intelligence and are certainly not perfect, but let's take a look at a summary. This is not a comprehensive list. I was not paid for these product mentions, nor am I responsible for their accuracy at the time of this reading.

Textio: analyzes the wording in both job descriptions and messaging with candidates and among teams, reveals the gender-coded language that you can't see, and suggests more inclusive language.

Greenhouse: allows you to anonymize candidate résumés; systemize candidate interview questions, and more.

Glider: provides real-work task assessments for candidates so they are evaluated on skill, rather than experience or background.

Entelo: anonymizes candidate résumés; allows you to specifically search for candidates who are underrepresented.

HireVue: provides structured video interviewing; provides real-work task assessments for candidates so they are evaluated on skill, rather than experience or background.

Pymetrics: provides game assessments for candidates so they are evaluated on skill, rather than experience or background.

Applied: scans job descriptions for overtly masculine or feminine language and suggests replacements; anonymizes candidate résumés; systemizes interview questions; provides real-work task assessments for candidates so they are evaluated on skill, rather than experience or background.

Inclusive 360 Action Steps

- ☐ Using the ARC Method*, analyze the entire hiring process for gaps and opportunities.
- ☐ Commit to solving for those gaps and include systems of accountability.
- ☐ Choose at least three new ways to expand your talent pipeline.
- ☐ Choose at least two ways to make the rest of your hiring process more fair.

Keep learning:

- Podcast: Codeswitch
- Podcast: Living Corporate

A LACK OF A DIVERSITY is a fixable problem. It takes intention to recruit underrepresented folks and to ensure your hiring process gives them a fair shot. Analyze your talent acquisition process by taking it through the ARC Method.

Ask better questions to establish your baseline diversity data, respect the answers you find, then connect to some of the meaningful solutions in this chapter.

CHAPTER 4

Start Me Up
Promoting Diversity

The broken rung

PROMOTING DIVERSITY CAN take many forms, but in this chapter, I'll focus on ways to amplify underrepresented voices within your organization.

The leadership of many organizations is not diverse. Leadership teams are often made up primarily of cisgender, white, straight men who unconsciously promote others like themselves. This is one type of unconscious bias that leads to a lack of diversity in higher levels of organizations.

In a McKinsey and LeanIn.Org survey of 329 companies, they found that for every 100 men promoted or hired at the manager level, only 72 women were hired or promoted to manager.

This "broken rung" happens very early on in the promotions process, often with women and BIPOC, and is the biggest obstacle to having diverse leadership. When these people don't get promoted out of entry level positions, they don't gain the experience and the track records to move up the ladder.

Because of the "broken rung," men end up with 62% percent of manager jobs while women hold just 38%. It's virtually impossible for women and BIPOC to catch up when they were left in the dust early on in their career.[60]

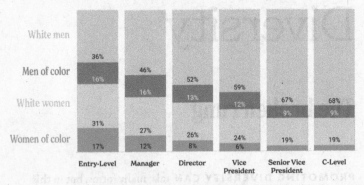

Corporate talent by gender and race:

Source: *Women in the Workplace 2018*, in which LeanIn.org and McKinsey examined the employee pipeline of 279 US corporations.

You can use the ARC Method° to guide your organization towards increased diversity at higher levels of the organization and ensuring underrepresented voices have a fair shot at being heard in the C-Suite and at events.

Follow the ARC to ask hard questions and analyze your organization's own processes. Again, this should be both a qualitative and quantitative exercise. This means asking leaders about their business objectives and looking for places to connect DEI initiatives to those goals. This also means you might have to ask the hard questions with underrepresented employees and truly listen to the experiences they have within the organization. You'll also have to dig into how leaders and managers make decisions. This data will be critical in creating a proactive step forward.

ASK.

- How do managers decide which employees get stretch assignments and exposure to leadership?
- How many underrepresented employees have we promoted at every level?
- How many of them received lateral moves? How many demotions?
- How does progress up the organization vary in speed by race? By gender?
- What happens when underrepresented employees attempt to move up in the organization?
- When our organization holds events (even virtual meetings), who speaks? Who sits on panels? What do those people look like?

Once you have some clarity on where you are, keep going!

RESPECT.

Respect the data you may find as you explore promotions. Respect the answers you hear when you talk to managers about the promotions process. Thoughtfully listen to the storytellers who bravely share their experiences at work—and respect the stories. Respect that this is process for change. Don't dismiss or hide the answers, even if you don't like what they tell you. Especially if you don't like what they tell you!

CONNECT.

Connect the answers to solutions—with accountability. And connect the accountability for solutions to leaders' assessments.

Success requires leaders to be held accountable for meeting diversity goals, and it requires having diversity and inclusion as standing agenda items. One form of accountability is through transparency, as research shows that people monitor their own biases when they expect that others will see what decisions they make.

A second form of accountability is through external monitoring, through which achieving diversity targets is part of a person's compensation and reward system.

Connecting your employees with each other for open conversations should be part of the solution, and other solutions may include some of the other strategies mentioned in the following sections of this chapter.

Publicly commit

Increasing leadership diversity within an organization never happens by accident because of built-in bias. Increasing diversity requires deliberate, intentional goals to which everyone in the organization is committed.

For example, several companies have taken intentional action and see substantial results especially around gender balance. NextRoll increased the number of women in senior management from 27% to 40%, Nordstrom increased the share of women in the C-suite from 7% to 40%, and Sodexo increased the number of women by more than 20% at the SVP level.[61]

What's the secret to this success? It starts with a public commitment to increasing diversity.

Unilever made a public commitment as well, that by 2021, its 14,000 global managers would be equally balanced between men and women. They achieved this goal in 2020.

Alan Jope, Unilever's chief executive, said: *"Women's equality is the single greatest unlock for social and economic development globally and having a gender-balanced workforce should be a given, not something that we aspire to."* [62]

Again, if you set such a target, you may hear grumblings from other employees who may wonder, "Did that person get promoted because they're a woman?"

Reassure them that your organization would not set itself up to fail by promoting a less-qualified candidate. It's simply not an option. I write about training employees in Chapter 11 but workshops can be effective at building allies (and reducing these complaints!).

The law firm Baker McKenzie set ambitious goals for gender balance in leadership: 40% men, 40% women, and 20% flexible (men, women, and/or non-binary). Recruitment pools achieved that balance in 2020 with firm-wide balance set for 2025. [63]

Over half of the 1,800+ Target stores in the U.S. are led by women. This is remarkable only because it doesn't happen by accident and shows leadership's commitment to celebrating diversity and reducing barriers to advancement.

According to Brian Cornell, Target's chairman and CEO, *"Leadership should reflect the customer you serve,"* and in Target's case, women do the bulk of the purchasing. *"Seventy-five percent of all retail purchases are made by women. They influence an even bigger percentage. We don't reflect that across the industry,"* Cornell added. *"We should have more diversity in the C-suite and more women as CEOs because she's the customer we're taking care of. Leadership should reflect the consumer you serve."*[64]

Unfortunately, Target's leadership is an exception, not the rule, but they've create a standard that other organizations should aspire to.

Restructure your promotions and performance review process

At Unilever, to achieve gender balance among its 14,000 managers worldwide, gender-balanced interview slate requirements were introduced.[65]

You may have heard this called the "Rooney Rule" which originated in the National Football League to increase the diversity of coaches. The rule is designed to mitigate unconscious bias by requiring teams to interview underrepresented candidates for coaching and office positions. You can do that within your own organization—require gender (and/or race) balanced slates of candidates for every open position, especially those in management. Keep the position open until you have those balanced slates.

As part of your promotions process, ensure that managerial candidates understand the organization's commitment to DEI. Then be sure to ask them questions about their own commitment to DEI! Below are some sample questions to ask managerial candidates:

- If you were to take steps to diversify your team, what would you not do?
- What have you done to ensure that coworkers feel a sense of belonging?

During employee performance reviews, it's important to provide as much structure as possible. Structured systems can mitigate the bias that shows up and prevents underrepresented talent from moving ahead in the organization.

Bias can show up here in all kinds of ways such as:

Familiarity bias aka: Like attracts like

> *Jordan just bought a starter home in my town. I remember buying my first home here. Jordan is like a younger me!*

> *Chris never stays late and never joins us for happy hour. Chris isn't a team player.*

Instead, focus on behavior and accomplishments. On your feedback forms, emphasize behaviors and accomplishments of your employees (over the past year)—not their personalities.

Recency bias aka: "What have you done for me lately?"

> *Morgan went above and beyond on that last project and is clearly all fives across the board.*

Solve for this by collecting data all year long, and holding performance reviews more than once per year. Many of the managers I speak with have a simple One Note file on each employee. If managers provide consistent feedback, the employee will be less likely to be shocked or offended by feedback that arises during the formal assessment.

Confirmation bias aka: Proving yourself right

> *Taylor's so great at project management and must be great at everything else, too.*

Instead, think like scientists. Seek out information that goes against what you already believe about an employee. For example, in this case, look specifically at other competencies you're measuring, and reflect on situations where Taylor may have room for growth.

Words matter

Rishi's accent is sometimes hard to understand.

Pat is so quiet and mustn't really care about this work.

Focus on each employee's message, not their style of communication. Multicultural employees often receive very general and unclear feedback on their communication styles, especially if they have an accent. Soft-spoken and/or introverted employees may be told to develop a more executive communication style to resonate better with clients.

As part of the process, employees should have the opportunity to self-evaluate using the same evaluation form their manager will use. That form should include structured criteria for feedback with specific close-ended questions. The scorecard should measure the employee on a scale that emphasizes competencies.[66]

One of my firm's clients uses the following rubric for assessments:

Below Standard (1): Shows little/no effort to work individually or with others; when work is initiated, it is often incomplete, with facts/key details omitted; work product and/or information sent to others often leads to confusion or inaction due to lack of clarity.

Developing (2): Interacts well across the team; makes an effort to self-initiate work product; output of work delivered is typically good, with relevant details included; work product often needs further development; effort and output may be below expectations at times.

Skilled (3): Interacts positively across the team; works to initiate own work product, often proactively; output of work delivered is well presented, inclusive of all relevant elements; quality is to standard; work effort and output match the expectations for the position.

Accomplished (4): Interacts positively across the team; works proactively to initiate work product, both required and unanticipated; output of work delivered is high quality, often including additional, unrequested elements; offers insight, work effort and output often above the expectations for the position.

Role Model (5): Proactively interacts positively at all levels; self-initiates work product, both required and unanticipated; work delivered is of the highest quality, including additional, unrequested elements; offers insight, leads work effort given expert-level knowledge; output typically above the expectation for the position.

I like this rubric because it describes very clearly the standards of each rating. It reduces the ambiguity that is directly correlated to bias.

Furthermore, the criteria that's assessed by the company is both job-focused and values-focused. The assessment specifically addresses the company's values such as:

- The employee makes sustainable choices in their day-to-day.
- The employee respects people and ideas in all their interactions.
- The employee seeks to improve continuously in their position.
- The employee strives to support our goal to succeed as one team.
- The employee is proactive and is engaged in our mission.

The more structure there is in your performance review process, the less likely it is that managers will fall into the trap of bias.

Another approach is to rewrite performance evaluation questions to be from the manager's perspective. For example:

If this person resigned, I would do anything to retain them
OR I would always want this person on my team
OR I would hire this person again.

This approach challenges managers to think more tactically about each employee's contributions to the team.

Create a sponsorship program

A core initiative to increase diversity in higher levels of organizations is sponsorship programs. This is a powerful, yet under-utilized, tool for retaining and promoting underrepresented talent.

Sponsors are powerful senior executives who directly enable their sponsees with career advancement and have a stake in their success. Simply put, sponsors use their personal clout to talk up and advocate for their sponsee to get promoted and develop more influence. To be most effective, sponsorship programs should be embedded in the DNA of the organizational culture.

Sponsorship programs are notably different from mentorship programs, which are typically focused more on sharing advice and resources. Mentors and mentees often have a casual relationship. While a mentor is someone who has knowledge and will share it with you, a sponsor is a person who has power and will use it for you. Sponsors and sponsees have a more structured and inclusive relationship.

Deloitte embedded sponsorship in its culture after a pilot program that paired women in a leadership training program with an executive sponsor. Within a year, nearly all participants had received promotions.

Now Deloitte has formalized an Emerging Leaders Development Program. This eight-month program connects high-potential managers from underrepresented groups to formal sponsors in senior leadership. Deloitte asks sponsees whom they would like as a sponsor, factoring in business line, growth opportunities, what gaps the sponsee has, and where they need visibility. Sponsors commit to at least a two-year relationship. [67]

You can start small when building a sponsorship program, even beginning with one department as a pilot. Ultimately, though, organizations must empower all department and team leaders to create sponsorship programs and provide the tools and resources to do so. Of course, not every senior leader will be an effective sponsor, and certainly not all will volunteer. Sponsors should be considered thoughtfully and provided with training to be successful.

As you create your Sponsorship program, follow the ARC.

ASK.

These are some of the questions you can Ask to set some intention behind your program:

- What criteria do we use to identify underrepresented talent to be sponsees?
- What criteria do we use to identify leaders who would be excellent sponsors?
- How do we hold sponsors accountable?
- What can we do to set the program up for success?
- How do we match sponsors and sponsees?

RESPECT.

Respect the voices that are in the room during these conversations. To launch a new initiative like this, you'll need the support of a lot of key stakeholders and will need to respect their voices—and the voices of underrepresented employees who can share their point of view of what success looks like.

CONNECT.

Connect the answers to specific solutions and criteria to establish a meaningful program. Connect those solutions and goals to systems of accountability that ensures the success of this program can be measured. Then connect individuals to each other.

Matching should connect sponsees with the people best suited to collaborate with them in a mutually beneficial and bidirectional relationship. There are pros and cons to matching sponsors and sponsees with people similar to themselves. If the sponsors and sponsees do have different backgrounds, set the sponsor up for success by training them on the challenges faced by underrepresented groups in the workplace.

Women are 50% less likely to have a sponsor in their careers than men. But of those that do, 85% of women continue to work full-time and strive for leadership roles relative to 58% of those without sponsors.

Only eight percent of people of color—9% of African-Americans, 8% of Asians and 5% of Hispanics—have a sponsor, compared to 13% of Caucasians. Increasing this number by building out a sponsorship program can make a significant impact in the overall organizational diversity makeup.[68]

Target's sponsorship program starts at the entry level. Mid-senior level executives are invited to a speed-networking like reception with the newly hired underrepresented populations. Executives and new hires meet individually to match up with goals and chemistry.[69]

Each year at Accenture, partners write out their personal objectives, part of which involves advancing diversity and inclusion. When sponsors complete their own self-assessments and are reviewed, they are also evaluated on their success as a sponsor. Similarly, the executives at Target are accountable to their Diversity Council direct report for the performance and advancement in the sponsorship program over a two-year period.[70]

Other organizations give sponsees the chance to request specific sponsors. Still others invite sponsors to purposefully seek out sponsees who have the track record, potential, and ambition to significantly contribute to the organization yet bring experiences and perspectives that are different from their own.

Communication boundaries, expectations, and goals are critical to establish at the beginning of the relationship. At the outset of your sponsorship program, also collect critical sponsee data (such as role within the company, involvement in committees, etc.) so adjustments can be made to the process and programs to fit the needs and growth of sponsees.

You can measure the impact of your sponsorship program by following the ARC. In addition to looking at hard data, consider using anonymous feedback mechanisms, including surveys, to collect information about the success of the program.

ASK.

These are some of the questions you can ask to evaluate your program:

- Are sponsees getting promoted?
- Are sponsees receiving improved feedback?
- What presented challenges? What could have been done differently?
- What is our biggest lesson learned?

RESPECT.

Respect the answers. Respect the data. Stay true. If underrepresented employees are not getting promoted, the sponsorship program is not working. If sponsees consistently receive constructive feedback, the program should be re-evaluated.

CONNECT.

Connect the answers to specific solutions and goals to improve the program. Connect those solutions and goals to systems of accountability to ensure underrepresented employees are actually getting promoted. Then again connect individuals to each other.

Perhaps you, dear reader, will consider not only creating a sponsorship program, but also being a sponsor yourself!

Hold everyone accountable

To be truly *Inclusive 360*, diversity, equity, and inclusion should be embedded into every aspect of your organization. As I've stated throughout, part of what it means to "Connect" when you follow the ARC, is to establish accountability systems. A key one is connecting DEI goals to performance assessments.

As part of accountability towards their gender balance in management goal, Unilever set a "gender appointment ratio," which measured the track records of senior leaders in appointing women.

Salesforce takes it a step further. Leaders who have more than 500 direct reports receive a diversity scorecard every month. The report tells the leaders:

1. The number and percentage of women and underrepresented minorities (Black, Latinx or Hispanic, American Indian/Native Alaskan, Hawaiian/Pacific Islander, and multiracial) in their organization
2. The number of women and underrepresented minorities who were hired into their organization in the previous month
3. The numbers of each who were promoted
4. The numbers of each who left the company

Molly Ford, Vice President of global equality programs at Salesforce, says, *"A leader can't say, 'Wow, I didn't promote a woman last year,' right?' You have the data in front of you. I want to give my executives the same rigor that they're looking at their pipeline or their sales numbers, the same rigor that they're looking at their people analytics data and dashboard."*

Quarterly scorecards are also issued for each leader, and those are shared with senior leaders in an operations review staff meeting.[71] This level of transparency ensures that everyone walks the talk.

Amplify voices

It's not only important to have a diverse workforce, but it's also important to ensure your organization consistently leads with diversity. One of the (many) places that lack diversity is events. Frequently, keynote speakers, moderators, and panelists are white, cisgender, and male, and often don't fully reflect the audience of their events. In fact, all-male panels have been given the adorable nickname *manels*.

Ensure there is diversity among any speakers you may have at your event, including race, gender, sexual orientation, age, etc. This requires significant intention and thoughtfulness, because when we have opportunities to give (such as speaking and panel opportunities), we often unconsciously choose people like us. Diversity doesn't happen by accident.

Cast a wide net when opening up a call for speakers. Share the opportunity within every network you can access and ask your employees to do the same. If you have Business Resource Groups (more on this in Chapter 10), ask members to share the speaking opportunities within their own personal networks.

Fortunately, there are some shining stars who model true diverse representation. Lesbians Who Tech is a massive tech conference where the speakers happen to be 80% **queer** women, 50% women of color, 25% Black and Latinx, and 10% transgender and/or non-binary people.[72]

It's intentional, and the conference is a huge success. It draws a massively diverse audience who are able to bring limitless points of view to important conversations around representation and inclusion in technology.

The Shoptalk 2021 Conference (postponed from 2020) has 225 speakers and all of them are women. The organizers are making a point this time around (over-correcting) but committing to 50/50 gender parity in speakers in 2022 and beyond.

Simran Rekhi Aggarwal, Founder and President of Shoptalk said in a statement. *"Is this all-female speaker approach extreme? Absolutely, but we think extreme problems require extreme solutions."* [73]

GenderAvenger.com is a blog and newsletter that tracks gender balance in all areas of public dialog, with a big focus on speaker representation. They call out events that lack diversity and even provide "stamps of approval" for events that embrace it. Connect with Gender Avenger if you're proud of your event's diversity and want a stamp of approval.

As a speaker myself, I've been most impressed when I've witnessed other speakers demand diversity. This takes courage and a willingness to take a stand. Some speakers have "inclusion riders" in their speaker contract, only agreeing to speak at events with speaker diversity. And some speakers have stepped down from speaking at homogenous events.

Dr. Francis Collins, a cisgender white man and the Director of the National Institutes of Health, stated that he will no longer speak on all-male panels to provide an opportunity for diverse voices. Dr. Collins is a great example of a person of privilege speaking out as a powerful ally.

Collins laid out his requirements in an announcement, published on June 12, 2019, titled "Time to End the Manel Tradition."

"Toward that end, I want to send a clear message of concern: it is time to end the tradition in science of all-male speaking panels, sometimes wryly referred to as 'manels.' Too often, women and members of other groups underrepresented in science are conspicuously missing in the marquee speaking slots at scientific meetings and other high-level conferences. Starting now, when I consider speaking invitations, I will expect a level playing field, where scientists of all backgrounds are evaluated fairly for speaking opportunities. If that attention to inclusiveness is not evident in the agenda, I will decline to take part. I challenge other scientific leaders across the biomedical enterprise to do the same." [74]

In 2019, several white male speakers publicly spoke out about the lack of diversity in the speaker lineup at the PHP Central Europe Conference (there was none), despite boasting a "rich and diverse lineup." The published schedule was criticized for including zero women. The event was canceled because numerous white male speakers declined their appearances in allyship with women.

Mark Baker, one of the speakers who decided to cancel his engagement, said *"It wasn't an easy decision to make, because I do enjoy sharing my coding passion; but having advocated for diversity at PHP developer conferences for the last several years, I have to follow my beliefs that diversity should be a cornerstone of the PHP developer community,"* Baker said. *"Diversity matters more to me than speaking."* [75]

This type of allyship matters because it forces conference organizers to be more inclusive, and the increased diversity of perspectives can then change the discussion in meaningful ways.

Organizations who lead with diversity and amplify the voices of underrepresented people at events send a signal to other people from underrepresented backgrounds that the organization is an attractive place to work. Furthermore, this commitment shows that an organization walks the talk and truly values diversity, equity, and inclusion. This is priceless and helps all levels of your organization.

Inclusive 360 Action Steps

☐ Using the ARC Method*, analyze the entire promotions process for gaps and opportunities.

☐ Commit to solving for those gaps and include systems of accountability.

☐ Make public commitments to specific numbers of underrepresented employees in leadership roles.

☐ Restructure the performance review process to mitigate bias.

☐ Establish a sponsorship program.

☐ Ensure every event you plan has diverse speakers, talent, and entertainment.

Keep learning:

- Book: Better Allies by Karen Catlin
- Book: The Inclusion Nudges Guidebook by Lisa Kepinski and Tinna C. Nielsen
- GenderAvenger www.genderavenger.com

FOLLOW THE ARC to ask hard questions and analyze your organization's own processes. This should be both a qualitative and quantitative exercise. This means asking leaders about their business objectives and looking for places to connect DEI initiatives to those goals. This also means you might have to ask the hard questions with underrepresented employees and truly listen to the experiences they have within the organization.

CHAPTER 5

True Colors
Every Voice
Matters

Increase your representation

IN 2020, STARBUCKS released an award-winning ad in the United Kingdom that tells the story of a transgender person with a buzz cut and nose ring who goes through life being misgendered and referred to by their "dead" name, Jemma (a "dead" name is the transgender person's name given at birth). That old name is used by a letter carrier, over a loudspeaker in a waiting room, and by the person's dad at a party.

The name was also on their ID card. The misgendering continues until they order their coffee at Starbucks, and they're asked for their name. "It's James," says the actor in the commercial. James's face lights up when the name is called out by the Starbucks barista.

In a press release, Starbucks said the ad, *"Was inspired by real-life experiences of people who were transitioning. We discovered that they found Starbucks stores to be a safe space, where their new name was accepted, and they could be (recognized) as who they are."* [76]

That, my friends, is representation. And that matters to not just transgender people, but all marginalized people. To feel seen and represented in media is not something that happens every day for people with marginalized identities.

In a similar move, the new face of Everlast Boxing is Patricio Manuel, who happens to be a transgender man. He is the first transgender boxer to compete professionally and is the star of Everlast's "Be First" campaign.

"At a time when transgender people are being questioned whether we have a place in the sporting world or even being recognized by the world at large, for Everlast to endorse me is huge," Manuel told CNN. *"It's a bold statement and I think it personifies the saying 'Be First.' I really hope it pushes other companies to think outside the box. This world is so incredibly diverse, we all deserve to have our identities and stories highlighted."*[77]

Representation doesn't mean adding the token Black person into a photo shoot. Authentic representation is about storytelling, about showing diverse folks as multi-dimensional. That's what matters.

Alan Jope, CEO of Unilever, pointed out that brands that engage in "woke-washing" by using the language and imagery of marginalized communities to increase sales, without actually advocating for those communities, should not be tolerated.

Jope added, *"Purpose-led brand communications is not just a matter of 'make them cry, make them buy.' It's about action in the world."*[78]

Heat, a Deloitte agency, studied the ads from 50 brands in eight industries over two years, and discovered that traditionally underrepresented people are increasingly visible in ads. Beyond that, those brands that feature the most people of color and women in ads averaged a 44% stock increase over those two years.[79]

In short, diverse representation matters to your bottom line. There are lots of ways you can expand diverse representation in your organization, but first you have to establish your baseline. You can do this by following the ARC.

ASK.

Ask the hard questions such as:

- When was the last time we held an employee listening session?
- Who are the artists whose works hang in our offices?
- What do the people in our marketing materials look like?
- Do our products represent and serve all people, including Black transgender women with disabilities?

RESPECT.

Respect the answers you find when you start reviewing your materials for diverse representation. Actively listen to the numbers and the data. Don't dismiss whatever you uncover, even if you don't like what you find. Especially if you don't like what you find!

Respect that this is process for change.

CONNECT.

Connect these answers to solutions where more of your customers and employees see themselves represented in your products and marketing. Connect your employees to each other to hold open conversations.

You can use the ARC Method® to guide your organization towards increased diversity.

Follow the ARC. Ask. Respect. Connect. Move from problem to solution.

Celebrate diversity

A "quick win" along your DEI journey is to celebrate some often overlooked religious, cultural, and racial holidays and use those as opportunities for educational programming. That's a great place to start, but make sure that's not where you end. Robust and thoughtful content should be provided all year long.

Ownership of these programs may start with Human Resources but should ultimately end up being driven by employee networks or resource groups (more on Business Resource Groups in Chapter 10).

Here are some of the more common dates for multicultural programming:

February: Black History/Heritage Month
March: Women's History Month
May: Asian Pacific American Heritage Month
June: LGBTQ+ Pride Month
September 15: National Hispanic Heritage Month begins
Second Monday in October: Indigenous People's Day
November: Native American Heritage Month
November 13–20: Transgender Awareness Week

Programming can take many forms. Here are just a few ideas:

- Lunch-and-learn workshops
- Film screening and discussion
- Book club
- Speakers
- Panel discussions
- Listening sessions like the ones I describe in Deep Dive, at the end of this section

Listen to your employees

Organizations are full of differences, and we all bring some of our personal baggage with us wherever we go. But underrepresented folks might bring trauma to work that's related to external factors, such as the hate crimes against Asian-Americans exacerbated by the COVID-19 pandemic; xenophobia experienced by Muslims after September 11 (and still); and shootings of Black people by police officers. It's hard for these folks to just leave that trauma at home. And with increasingly blurry lines between home and work, the workplace must become a place where conversations around these topics are safe.

Many organizations began their journey towards antiracism and racial justice when George Floyd was murdered by a Minneapolis police officer in May 2020. One organization after the other made public condemnations of the murder and public commitments to antiracism. It was about time.

While it took until 2020 for many organizations to make public condemnations and commitments, several years earlier, after an innocent Black man named Botham Jean was killed by police in Dallas, PriceWaterhouse Coopers (PwC) launched Courageous Conversations. Jean was a PwC employee. Courageous Conversations is a facilitated forum/listening series where employees can address difficult issues, hear diverse perspectives, share their own perspectives, and say what needs to be said. The initiative was spearheaded by PwC Chairman, Tim Ryan.

Courageous Conversation participants must attend and commit to six actions: Be open, authentic, engaged, comfortable being uncomfortable, non-judgmental, and understanding. The goal is to create brave environments for open, honest, and respectful dialogue.

"These conversations are not easy and sometimes uncomfortable," Ryan wrote in an email, which he shared with HuffPost. *"But one thing I've heard this week is that it's also uncomfortable when the issues that are on the top of our minds are not part of the conversation at work."*

The first Courageous Conversation was around race, with a goal to equip the workforce with the skills and techniques to have effective conversations in the workplace around topics that may be outside of their comfort zone. Other topics have included gender dynamics, LGBTQ+ inclusion, current events, and more.

"Discussing these types of difficult topics is usually assumed to be the responsibility of community leaders, politicians, and activists," Ryan wrote on LinkedIn. *"But our people spend a good portion of their lives within the walls of this firm and more than anything, I want them to be able to bring their whole selves to work."* [80]

Since PwC's precedent, hundreds of other organizations, large and small, have hosted facilitated listening series.

These sessions can help your organization gather qualitative data that you can combine with any quantitative assessments to establish a baseline for your DEI initiatives. A trained facilitator can be valuable for these sessions so that you don't burden underrepresented talent with the emotional labor/possible re-traumatization of facilitating these sessions themselves.

Deep Dive

LISTENING SESSIONS

If you do hold these listening sessions yourself, here are some tips to make sure they have a lasting impact:

1. Create ground rules (including what happens when someone says the "wrong" thing) around how to discuss racism and Black Lives Matter (if that's what your specific topic is). Provide common language, which could include sharing the DEI glossary at the end of this book, to alleviate fear around saying the wrong thing.

2. Create learning environments that center (focus on) the experience of the particular employee group you're discussing, and only their experience. For example, if it's a conversation around the Black employee experience, and white defensiveness/fragility emerges, recenter the Black experience. Always bring it back to that. If you have a white employee who is really struggling to center the Black experience, use the ARC Method* to ask great questions (the allyship version described in Chapter 1).

3. Curate learning resources, including facts on systemic racism, for your employees so that they can self-educate.

4. Follow up with training to enhance your employees' skills to actively listen, engage, and process conversations about race and equity.

5. Follow up listening sessions with dedicated working sessions for senior leaders to identify action steps and identify deeper level training required.

6. Consider reverse mentoring or upskilling programs where leaders can learn from their employees.

7. Follow up these listening sessions with actual systems changes (there are many ideas in this book!) to further your commitment to DEI.

Include diverse representation in marketing

Showcasing diversity is best practice for any business. The more diversity a brand showcases, not just in its marketing, but even throughout its website, the more diverse employees and customers they are likely to attract. Showcasing diversity makes others feel more welcome and included. It provides "possibility models," especially to underrepresented people who don't often see themselves in ads.

In 2020, Altra Running announced a sponsorship of two new athletes—and they're both pregnant women. These runners appear in Altra ads, but unlike other brands, they're not required to compete a specific number of times or to medal in order to keep their sponsorship. The package Altra athletes Alysia Montaño and Tina Muir receive includes financial compensation and shoes in exchange for press appearances. This decision by Altra sets a new standard in an industry with a reputation for penalizing pregnant women. [81]

Montaño's former sponsor, Asics, reduced her pay and later withdrew financial support during a previous pregnancy. She hopes that being open about the issues mothers face, both within and outside the world of sports, will help companies understand these problems and work toward solutions like robust maternity policies.

More brands are also paying attention to the importance of plus-size inclusion. In 2019, the Nike Store in London displayed new mannequins representing diverse body types.[82] Shoppers loved the parasport and curvy mannequins, which show that there's more than one way to be athletic.

Similarly, both Old Navy and Nordstrom started using curvy mannequins as well. Missguided, a British fashion brand, even used mannequins from diverse ethnic groups, some of whom rocked stretch marks, freckles, and vitiligo. These are people and characteristics that are almost never reflected in marketing. It's powerful to finally see them reflected in promotions!

Procter & Gamble was celebrated for several of their commercials: "The Talk," which showcased Black parents explaining the realities of racial bias to their kids over time was well supported. The company went on to produce "The Look," which shows a day in the life of a Black man, and his experiences with microaggressions and profiling. Both commercials beautifully (and painfully) illustrate common Black experiences in America and build more awareness and empathy among well-meaning people who might not otherwise have this exposure. [83]

Mapbox was disappointed in the lack of representation of queer folks in stock photos, and as a tech company, particularly wanted to see queer folks represented in tech. Because of this, Mapbox created a collection of free stock photos of queer people in tech that is available for everyone to access.

In its blog post, Mapbox says, *"We created this photo set to promote the visibility of queer and gender-nonconforming (GNC) people in technology, who are often underrepresented as workers powering the creative, technical, and business leadership of groundbreaking tech companies and products. We created these images to encourage and enable everyone in tech to represent LGBTQIA+ people at work."* [84]

VICE.com also launched their own free set of transgender and non-binary stock photos as well, with images of folks playing video games, visiting the doctor's office, and living life. Many of these people are of color, and therefore have intersectional marginalized identities. [85]

If you've ever searched stock photos for images of hands holding a phone or typing, you may have discovered that the hands in the photos are usually white. Nappy, a free stock photo site with beautiful images of Black and brown people, released a new "All Hands" collection, specifically showcasing Black and brown hands using personal computing devices. Nappy also committed to representing accessibility, gender fluidity, age, and body positivity in the photos. [86]

Adding one of these photos to slide decks your employees use, or your website's "Careers" section would be a simple thing you can do to demonstrate that you care about inclusion. It will fall flat, however, unless you also commit to walking the talk and creating a great employee culture that fulfills the promise you make in your marketing.

Increase diverse representation in product design

In 2004, Massachusetts became the first state in the country to have marriage equality for same-sex couples. Slowly, more and more states began to follow suit, while others offered civil unions. Thousands of same-sex couples were getting married.

Despite these shifts, there was one perpetual challenge for the loving guests attending those weddings: they couldn't find non-gendered greeting cards (i.e., cards that didn't say "bride" and "groom" or "husband" and "wife") in brick and mortar stores. There was typically only one option, if that. As a wedding planner at the time, I heard stories of guests who were late to the wedding because they put off getting a card until the last minute, and then couldn't find anything non-gendered!

Guests often had to order cards online and the selection back then was limited. Hallmark didn't begin to release cards for these couples until late 2008, and even then, they were not widely available. But they are now.

Representation helps people feel seen, and this is particularly important for children.

American Girl Dolls for Girl's 2020 Girl of the Year has congenital hearing loss. Approximately 15% of children have hearing loss, and this is the first time an American Girl doll has been produced with a physical disability. This doll comes with a removable hearing aid.

"We've long offered dolls and accessories that speak to girls in a variety of circumstances and Joss is another great example of how we celebrate inclusivity," Julie Parks, a spokesperson for the company said. *"Having a character with a disability is something we know girls and moms were interested in reading about."* [87]

In 2019, Sesame Street introduced a muppet named Karli, who is in foster care. Karli has a parent battling addiction. The storyline is told from Karli's perspective, unlike any other programming around addiction. It's a powerful way to be inclusive of the diversity of experiences that can affect kids.

"There's nothing else out there that addresses substance abuse for young, young kids from their perspective," said Kama Einhorn, a senior content manager with Sesame Workshop.

Sesame Street hired children's therapist Jerry Moe, from the Hazelden Betty Ford Children's Program, to craft the segments featuring Karli.

"These boys and girls are the first to get hurt and, unfortunately, the last to get help," Moe said. *"For them to see Karli and learn that it's not their fault and this stuff is hard to talk about and it's OK to have these feelings, that's important. And that there's hope."* [88]

In 2019, Mattel introduced Creatable World, a new doll with no obvious gender. It includes interchangeable hairstyles and clothing that is neither masculine nor feminine. This doll can be a boy, a girl, neither, or both a boy and a girl. The product's slogan is "A doll line designed to keep labels out and invite everyone in."

"There were a couple of gender-creative kids who told us that they dreaded Christmas Day because they knew whatever they got under the Christmas tree, it wasn't made for them," says Monica Dreger, head of consumer insights at Mattel. *"This is the first doll that you can find under the tree and see is for them because it can be for anyone."*

A study by the Williams Institute at the University of California, Los Angeles, found that 27% of California teens identify as gender-nonconforming. And a 2018 Pew study found 35% of Gen Z-ers (born 1995 to 2015) say they personally know someone who uses gender-neutral pronouns like they and them. With more kids who see gender beyond the binary, this doll is a game changer.[89]

If you have a smartphone, you may have noticed that emojis have become increasingly inclusive. More recent emojis include a person in a motorized wheelchair, a probing cane, a mechanical leg, and an ear with a hearing aid. There are also holding hands emojis with any shade of skin tone, and also transgender flags, the transgender symbol, and more. These inclusive emojis are a great example of making sure that their product is mindful of all different types of people and lets everyone's voice shine.

Video game developer DONTNOD Entertainment introduced the game *Tell Me Why* in 2019. The title features a playable main character, Tyler Ronan, who happens to be a transgender man. Game director Florent Guillaume and Joseph Staten, senior creative director at Xbox, wanted to ensure they authentically represented the trans experience and hired a transgender actor, August Black, to voice the character. They also consulted with LGBTQ+ media organization, GLAAD, on accurate representation.[90]

The hope is for players to identify with Tyler for his humanity. Guillaume says, *"Tyler is a young man with great values, good and bad [elements], that's what makes him human."*

When creating any products, consider the audience and how you can represent the vast diversity of your potential audience. You will find that you're more authentically able to represent that diversity when you have broad perspectives in the rooms where these ideas come to life. You cannot create authentic portrayals without conversations with members of the communities you're trying to represent.

Amplify underrepresented folks in art

A couple of museums corrected decades of curating art from mostly white male artists. In 2020, the Baltimore Museum of Art committed to only purchasing art (including paintings, sculptures, and ceramics) from female artists (including transgender women). In 2020, all of their 22 exhibits had a female-centric focus.

In making this commitment, Museum Director Christopher Bedford said, *"You don't just purchase one painting by a female artist of color and hang it on the wall next to a painting by Mark Rothko. To rectify centuries of imbalance, you have to do something radical."* [91]

In a similar move, the San Francisco Museum of Modern Art also showed they care about showcasing diverse artists. The museum sold Rothko's Untitled and then purchased works by female and minority artists Rebecca Belmore, Forrest Bess, Frank Bowling, Leonora Carrington, Lygia Clark, Norman Lewis, Barry McGee, Kay Sage, Alma Thomas, and Mickalene Thomas. The remaining proceeds from the Rothko sale will be used to establish an endowment fund for future acquisitions. [92]

Country Music Television (CMT) made a commitment to play music videos from male and female artists equally. This may seem like a no-brainer, but country music radio previously played 87% male artists, so this commitment from CMT is significant. More air time = more music and ticket purchases = more money in the hands of female artists. [93]

Now, most organizations probably don't have their own museum or gallery or music channel. But some may have the works of artists hanging in their offices. Some have their own organizational podcasts. Look for ways to amplify underrepresented voices in those mediums.

Take responsibility and give credit to marginalized people

In 2020, the Kansas City Star newspaper issued an editorial apologizing for decades of unfair and overlooked coverage of the Black community. Among other things, the paper failed to cover bombings of Black homes in the city and provided poor coverage of local legends Jackie Robinson and Charlie Parker.

The editorial reads, in part: *"Through sins of both commission and omission—it disenfranchised, ignored and scorned generations of Black Kansas Citians. It reinforced Jim Crow laws and redlining. Decade after early decade it robbed an entire community of opportunity, dignity, justice and recognition."* [94]

This matters because racial justice includes taking ownership for past mistakes, even ones that are "not our fault." It also includes making commitments and righting wrongs, as the Star did, in part by hiring an editor to address race issues, and by covering stories of systemic racism, Black Lives Matter, and more. The Kansas City Star took responsibility.

In 2020, NASA renamed its Washington, D.C. headquarters after Black engineer Mary W. Jackson. This matters because this prominent building provides Black visibility and amplifies, rather than erases, Black contributions to American history. NASA gave proper credit to a woman who earned it. [96]

Major League Baseball (MLB) corrected history by giving the Negro League full Major League Baseball Status. Players like Willie Mays will now have their Negro League records count towards their MLB total. This is long overdue, but it's now done, and the players will get credit. Now, they will be amplified and given the credit that they deserve. [97]

IBM Makes It Right

Another example of a company taking responsibility is the case of Lynn Conway who was an innovative computer scientist at IBM when she was fired in 1968 after coming out as transgender. The job loss turned her life upside down. In October 2020, 52 years later, IBM genuinely apologized, acknowledged her legacy at the company and awarded her a Lifetime Achievement Award.

"I wanted to say to you here today, Lynn, for that experience in our company 52 years ago and all the hardships that followed, I am truly sorry," Diane Gherson, a former Senior Vice President said at the event.

Gherson went on to describe IBM's best-in-class LGBTQ+ inclusive policies and added to Conway, *"I'm confident in saying... you would have been treated quite differently today. But all that doesn't help you, Lynn.... So, we're here today not only to celebrate you as a world-renowned innovator and IBM alum, but also to learn from you, and by doing so, create a more inclusive workplace and society."* [95]

This matters because it sets a great example of corporate vulnerability. It matters in particular to LGBTQ+ employees at IBM. IBM took responsibility and is making sure that the mistakes that were made in the past don't happen again.

Are there places in your organization's history where there was injustice, where credit was misgiven? It's never too late to apologize and set the record straight. Committing to DEI means addressing past mistakes. They are never easy to bring up, but they are necessary to show that your company is truly committed to being inclusive and standing up for its underrepresented employees.

Inclusive 360 Action Steps

☐ Using the ARC Method*, analyze your products.

☐ Commit to solving for those gaps and include systems of accountability.

☐ Create at least one educational program during at least four different diversity months or weeks.

☐ Establish thoughtfully organized listening sessions, starting with conversations around the Black employee experience.

☐ Look for opportunities to showcase diverse artists within your offices and/or at your events.

☐ Examine your marketing and create a diversity checklist as part of all new marketing campaigns. In what other ways can your marketing reflect diversity? Identity one way to make your marketing better reflect the diversity of our world.

☐ Explore your products and create a diversity checklist as part of all new product development. In what other ways can your products reflect diversity? Identify one way to make your products better reflect the diversity of our world.

☐ Look for decisions in the organization's past that may have been unjust. Apologize and make it right.

Keep learning:

- Book: Empowering Differences by Ashley Brundage
- Book: You are Enough! by Charlene Wheeless
- Book: Belonging at Work by Rhodes Perry

Part 2:
EQUITY

CHAPTER 6

Sign O' the Times
Understanding Equity

Define equity

YOU MAY HAVE SEEN IT—the graphic of three kids of different heights trying to watch the baseball game over the fence. There is one tall kid that can see over the fence just fine, one that is about medium height that just barely can see over, and one short kid that can't see over the fence at all. If the kids are treated equally and receive equal boxes, the shorter kid still can't see over. If treated equitably, the shorter kids receive the appropriate-sized box to stand on so they can all see over the fence. Each kid is given a fair shot based on their own unique circumstances, in this case, their height.

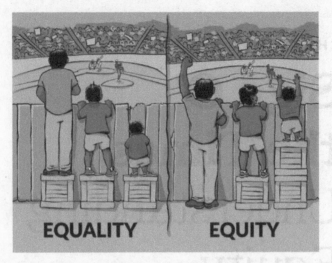

Figure 1: Interaction Institute for Social Change | Artist: Angus Maguire.

Equality ("the condition of being equal") simply isn't possible without equity ("more for those who need it") first. Equality is not possible without equitable systems that attempt to make up for our universal legacy of white supremacy, racism, sexism, homophobia, and transphobia.

Right now, and for a long time to come, equity is much more important than equality. It's not possible to achieve the holy grail of "equality" without first giving more to those who need it. Equality is not possible without equity.

Equity involves changing the systems of law, leadership, human resources, and virtually everything else. For years, centuries even, systems were made by those in power (usually those of the dominant race, gender, class, religion, and sexual orientation—usually straight, white men) to keep themselves (and people like them) in power.

Here are some examples of inequity from the United States that you may not realize.

- White women couldn't vote until 1920.
- Black people couldn't vote until 1965.

- Segregation wasn't legally ended until 1964.
- Interracial marriage was illegal until 1967.
- Black people were excluded from certain sections of cities until 1968. [98]
- In 28 states, LGBTQ+ people (or those assumed to be) could be legally fired from their job based on their sexual orientation or gender identity until 2020.
- LGBTQ+ people can still be denied housing or access to public accommodations in 28 states as of publication, the ones that are gray in the map below. [99]

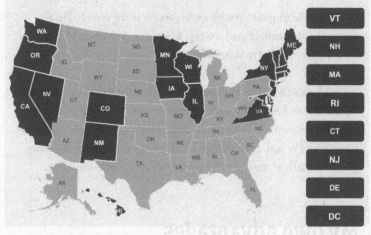

U.S. Anti-Discrimination Laws

Black states on this map provide statewide discrimination protections on the basis of gender and sexual orientation.

These are some examples of how the "system was rigged" to keep powerful people in power. Those rigged systems gave white men a huge head start on professional opportunities. As a result, these rigged systems created generations of wealth for white men, while others were legally held back. It will take decades, centuries even, for marginalized people to catch up to where white men are in terms of their status. Meritocracy, or the belief that success is based exclusively on skill or talent, is a fallacy. Success is much harder to achieve for those who have experienced centuries of inequity.

The result of centuries of inequity is that, despite those laws protecting against racial discrimination at work, in housing, and other economic realms, the average white household has about seven times more wealth than the average Black household. Distribution of wealth hasn't changed much since the civil rights movement. [100]

Equity challenges us to fix the systems in order to give everyone a fair shot. Not only fix the systems so that future generations have a great chance at equality, but to fix the systems to make up for *all of the inequities* of the past.

Now, you may be like me and say:

"Well, I didn't grow up with a silver spoon in my mouth. I'm a first-generation college grad. I worked hard for everything I have! Why should I get involved in this stuff?"

I'm a lesbian who speaks about diversity and inclusion, works in this field, and have been on my own journey towards realizing my own privilege and my own role as an ally to those who have even fewer opportunities than I've had. Even though I had immigrant parents who struggled financially at times, I still have the advantage of being white.

My own advantages

I didn't invent slavery. I wasn't there on the plantation. I'm not even from the South.

But I benefited from slavery. It kept white people in charge, and my white family never experienced the trauma of seeing proud Confederate flags and Robert E. Lee statues on display, despite what those images represent.

I wasn't even born in the 1930s. I hadn't even heard of redlining until 20 years ago. It's not my fault Black people were prevented from buy-

ing homes because banks wouldn't offer loans when the government la-
beled Black neighborhoods as risky investments.

But I still benefited from this because my family members were all
able to buy homes, and those homes became investments in our future.
Later, when I bought my first home, it was in a gentrifying neighborhood, and it was from a Black woman about to go into foreclosure. I
benefited from redlining.

In the 1980s, I was just a kid. I didn't know anyone doing crack or
cocaine. It's not my fault the prison sentence for crack (a primarily poor
Black drug) was 100 times more strict than the prison sentence for cocaine (a primarily rich white drug), even though the drugs are from the
same plant. It's not my fault that this led to millions of young Black
men in jail, effectively enslaving them and forcing them to leave their
families behind.

But I benefited from the "war on drugs," because cops were so focused on arresting young Black men that they let me go when, at the
age of 19, I ran a red light with six people in my Chrysler which reeked
of marijuana.

I've never worked for the electoral system or any government. I've
never been a poll worker. I've never had trouble voting. It's not my
fault thousands of Black voters have trouble voting. It's not my fault
their names are removed from voter roll or their polling places close
early, or they're given the wrong ballot, or their state doesn't allow
felons to vote.

But I benefited from voter suppression because it didn't happen to
me. This meant that I never once questioned my ability to participate
fully in a democracy.

I had a Black girlfriend once, whom I'll refer to as M. She came with
me to my aunt's restaurant in upstate New York. We sat at the bar. She
got some dirty looks. I didn't notice. She felt unsafe. I didn't notice. As
we drove away, she told me what she experienced. We almost broke up

because I simply didn't get it. We did break up, eventually, but I wasn't the one giving dirty looks. It wasn't my fault.

Right?

Wrong.

I benefited from never knowing how she felt. In fact, I benefit every day from feeling safe almost everywhere because most people, especially those in power, look like me. I benefit every day from not being followed around stores or having my résumé ignored because of my name. I benefit every day because my professional qualifications are not questioned due to my race. I benefit every day because there are grocery stores with fresh produce in my neighborhood.

I benefit every day because I'm not two and a half times more likely to be killed by the police.

I benefit every day because I'm white. That's white privilege, which has been built up from centuries of white supremacy ideology interwoven within every system in this country.

> Slavery was not my fault, but I benefited,
> so it's my responsibility.
> Redlining is not my fault, but I benefit,
> so it's my responsibility.
> The war on drugs is not my fault, but I benefit,
> so it's my responsibility.
> Voter suppression is not my fault, but I benefit,
> so it's my responsibility.
> What happened with M was not my fault, but I was ignorant,
> so it's my responsibility.

I didn't invent these (or any of the many other) systems of inequality. But I benefit from them. Therefore, it's my responsibility to help dismantle them.

If you are a white person like me, I hope you will see that racial equity is all of our responsibility. It's unreasonable to expect those who suffer from our systems of white supremacy to do the work to dismantle them.

How does this inequity play out in organizations? The short story is that organizational systems mirror society. Powerful people (and those who look like them) tend to stay in charge and have power.

Identify your systems

The work to dismantle systems of white supremacy and inequity can take many forms but starts with recognizing our own systems of influence or control, the areas in which we hold some power. Each of us influences or controls some system. In the workplace, perhaps you influence or control some aspect of the hiring process, promotions process, or purchasing/procurement process. Maybe you sit on a committee or a Board of Directors.

In your personal life, perhaps you influence some aspect of an organization of which you're a member, a church or volunteer group. Maybe you influence members of your family. You certainly have influence or control over your friend group and/or professional network.

Virtually every human has some degree of influence, control, or power. Start with identifying the systems in which you have power, influence, or control.

Now, look closely at those systems. Where are there opportunities to make small changes in order to expand access to those systems? To make them more equitable?

Certainly, there are changes which can be made in hiring processes to attract more underrepresented talent to your organization (I wrote about this in Chapter 3). But it goes beyond that.

Dismantling systems of white supremacy and racism starts with using our own influence, control, or power to give others a fair shot. This doesn't mean taking away opportunities from other people. It means making a bigger pie, where there's a slice for everyone. It doesn't mean that those of us with power and privilege get less pie when others start to finally get a slice.

The pie expands.

Don't you love pie? Or cake? (Or insert your favorite baked treat....)

In the Diversity section, I wrote about increasing diversity by expanding access to employment opportunities for underrepresented talent. Equity asks us to fix the rigged systems so that those underrepresented employees get a fair shot to succeed and recover from generations of unequal access.

I have no doubt that you may receive some push-back from those who think and see these strategies as giving Black and other underrepresented talent an unfair advantage. Creating a more equitable system doesn't give underrepresented talent an unfair advantage, instead it creates an even playing field where everyone is treated equally. The reality is that we've come to see the lack of equity as normal, as appropriate. Bias is deeply imbedded in every aspect of the workplace.

Equity is about acknowledging that bias is harmful to underrepresented people, protecting them, and fixing the systems to correct the injustice.

Inclusive 360 Action Steps

☐ Reflect on your own experiences with race and privilege. Consider how you may have benefited from others' lack of equity.

☐ Identify your own systems of influence and control.

☐ Examine ways to expand access to your own systems.

Keep learning:

- Book: Stamped from the Beginning by Ibram X. Kendi
- Movement Advancement Project: www.LGBTMap.org

CHAPTER 7:

What's Going On
Racial Justice

Move towards becoming an antiracist organization

IN THE AFTERMATH of the murders of George Floyd, Breonna Taylor, and other Black people killed by police in 2020, racial justice and racial equity became hot topics in the United States. People were finally starting to realize that Black people have had a much different lived experience than everyone else. And for the first time, thousands of organizations began publicly supporting the Black Lives Matter movement, a movement that has been fighting for the equal treatment of BIPOC.

Many were also starting to talk about antiracism, a term popularized by Professor Ibram X. Kendi. Antiracism is described as the consistent practice of questioning and dismantling systems of racism. Because, as Kendi writes, *"Racial inequity is a problem of bad policy, not bad people."*[101]

The good news is that policies can be changed to be more just. In fact, there are lots of policies that can be changed within organizations to be more equitable—to be antiracist.

But first, your leadership team must be in sync on a few key things:

- How to issue statements around social and political issues
- How to respond to conservative leaning employees who complain they no longer feel "safe"
- What is meant by "systemic inequities," "inclusive culture," "diverse team," "antiracist," or any other buzzwords used in communications

Unfortunately, with how things are now, there will be more police violence and police killing of Black people like George Floyd and Breonna Taylor. There will be more calls for accountability. The next time that happens, will you stand up for your Black, Asian, Latinx, or other affected employees and go beyond words to change the systems and truly build an antiracist organization?

Here's how to start when a community is impacted by a traumatic event. In this section, I'll be referencing Black employees, but you can follow the same ideas and actions to support other underrepresented employees as well.

1. Talk about it externally, and especially internally.

Your organization should issue some statement that recognizes that Black employees are likely feeling grief, exhaustion, and fear. Start with an internal statement to establish your credibility and commitment. The statement may mention that many non-Black employees want to help, but they don't know how to. Statements should always focus on Black people/employees and not diminish their experience by lumping them in with anyone else affected. Statements that show support for Black employees in one breath, and then empathize with those whose homes were damaged by looters (following the racial justice uprisings) in the next breath, diminish the experience of Black folks.

Ensure those statements include specific antiracist policy commitments (there are many examples in this book related to hiring, promotions, procurement, and more). Either acknowledge the policy changes you've made or specify the ones you're publicly committing to—beyond just donating some money to a Black organization.

If you don't make specific policy commitments, you're going to get some major push back such as:

"If Black Lives Matter, then why doesn't our leadership team have any Black people?"

"Great, another organization that sends its thoughts and prayers instead of action."

Statements and words aren't enough—you have to make policy commitments.

Upwork Shows How It's Done

Upwork's CEO, Hayden Brown wrote an internal memo to employees that is a great example of one that expresses outrage, empathy, and specific commitment. It reads, in part:

I couldn't let today go by without acknowledging the breaking news about George Floyd's unnecessary death in police custody in Minnesota. The news is yet another devastating blow to our national identity and something that should unify us in outrage. The violence must stop. The dehumanization must stop. We need to stand together against this inexcusable racist, violent behavior.

I want to emphasize our continued commitment at Upwork to creating a safe environment for honest conversations about race, about these painful acts, and about how we can support each other through these traumatic events and through the persistent racism that many of you experience ev-

ery day. Our Leadership Team takes this seriously. We have committed to a number of actions in support of allyship and towards building a diverse and inclusive workplace for everyone, including our Black team members. Our commitments include quarterly data deep dives to unpack how we are doing against our diversity goals, active participation in and hosting of intimate conversations with our BIN BRG and Black employees, and setting and holding ourselves accountable to measurable goals around Black leader hiring and Black team member promotion rates. We have real work to do here at Upwork to address high Black employee attrition rates, low representation of Blacks in our workforce, and underrepresentation of Blacks in leadership positions, I want you to know that we are committed to addressing these issues. [102]

If you want to take it a step further, then call out the elephant in the room, just as Ben and Jerry's did in a public letter after George Floyd's murder. [103] The headline read:

Dismantle White Supremacy.
Silence is not an option.

The letter continued with four major calls to legislative action. The company also has racial justice education on its website and addresses racism in America on its podcast.

2. Keep listening. Keep the conversation going.

Create spaces for Black voices to be heard. Host listening sessions (facilitated by a third party, to reduce the emotional labor on Black employees) as I discussed on page 91.

Cadillac held fireside chats between Black employees and executives, and that evolved into workshops, and then a storytelling series. Storytelling series could and should include stories of triumph and celebration, not just stories of Black adversity and inequity. [104]

Managers can make a direct impact by leading with vulnerability and authenticity and asking themselves questions like:

- What can I take off my over-burdened employees plates?
- What can I alleviate from my Black team members who have been carrying an emotional weight in professional circles for some time?

I recommend that you require managers to check in one-on-one with their Black employees after any kind of incident of racial trauma. Give your managers some conversation starters and tools on empathetic listening. When opening a meeting in the wake of a traumatic racial incident, it's important managers acknowledge what happened. Here's a sample conversation starter for a meeting:

"Before we get started today, I want to recognize that the world feels unjust, and acknowledge the terrible trauma experienced by our Black colleagues, friends, and family. I'd like to take a moment and invite you to consider how you're feeling right now, and if there's anything that is holding you back from being fully present in this meeting. Feel free to share if you'd like, or we can just pause for a bit before we get started. Of course, you can take some time and sign off, if you need to."

In check-ins with Black employees, white managers might not know what to say. Follow the ARC Method° for sample conversation starters.

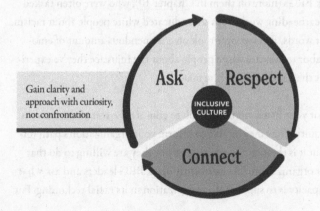

ASK.

- What can I do to best support you?
- Are you feeling seen and supported as an individual here at the organization?
- Do you mind telling me more about your experience as a Black person at our organization?

Now, you might find that folks prefer not to talk about this stuff at work, and that's OK. Everyone has their own process for dealing with grief. You can simply let your employee know that you are a resource for them, and they have the full support of the organization.

RESPECT and CONNECT.

Listen empathetically and respect whatever answers you receive and connect to real solutions if you can. Connecting to solutions does not necessarily mean "fixing" the problem or being the "savior." Connecting can simply be about validating the employee and ensuring they feel heard. Let them take the lead on what they need from you and what you can do for them.

3. Support Black Business Resource Groups (BRGs).

During the racial justice conversations of 2020, I heard from colleagues in Black BRGs (more on them in Chapter 10), who were often tasked with spearheading workshops that educated white people about racism. In other words, Black people took on a tremendous amount of emotional labor to educate white people about the injustice they've experienced at the hands of the white majority.

It's not your Black employees' job to educate the rest of the crew on racial equity. They may be able to inform your organization's path forward, but it is their choice whether or not they are willing to do that for your organization. Check in with Black BRG leaders and ask what their capacity is to support the organization in its racial reckoning. For most Black employees at your organization, even the BRG leaders, it's not their job to lead your organization towards racial justice. White people have to do that work themselves.

I highly recommend that you bring in an external facilitator or consultant as you begin to host Courageous Conversations, antiracism workshops, unconscious bias trainings, and address other equity topics.

4. Look for other places racism might show up in your product design, marketing, or vendor relationships.

A simple example of subtle racial trauma comes from the wedding industry. Many popular wedding venues in the South are former slave plantations, and the weddings hosted there are often described as "charming" and "elegant" on wedding blogs and sites. Major companies in the wedding industry agreed to stop promoting weddings at these plantations, as they recognized the historical context of these lands. Some, such as Zola and Pinterest, won't accept advertising from those venues, either, and while that's a step in the right direction, there's more work to be done.[105]

A few years ago, H&M clothing put a young Black child model in a sweatshirt that read "coolest monkey in the jungle." If you're not familiar, "monkey" is a racist term for Black folks.

I don't know whether there were any Black people involved when they were casting the actors or designing the product. Maybe there wasn't a Black person involved when they were on set, shooting the model. Maybe no Black people were involved with the graphic design. Maybe there was a lack of diversity, which led to the employees who were involved simply not understanding how to avoid unintentionally offending H&M's Black customers.

Maybe there was one or more Black people in some of those rooms. And maybe that Black person did not feel safe speaking up, because they were afraid of retribution. They were afraid of retaliation. Maybe they just didn't feel like their voices actually mattered, so they chose to remain silent.

It doesn't matter. The results, the impact of this, was significant for H&M. They deeply offended and traumatized Black customers and lost the endorsement of the Weeknd, a huge pop singer. This ad had an immediate backlash.[106]

Since then, H&M created some new systems to ensure this never happens in the future. Their new process includes:

- At least 12 people in the studio see a photo after it is uploaded
- Clothing can be flagged at every stage and notes about sensitivities can be made
- Five people do final-round quality checks (up from one)

They changed the systems to reduce the risk of this happening in the future.

5. Leverage your personal systems.

Individuals can be antiracist, too. Most people have systems that we can influence and we can control. At work you may be part of a committee. You may be part of an organization, a board that you sit on, or a volunteer at a local nonprofit or church. Even your family system can be an area you influence.

How can you use your unearned advantages to invite people who are different from you to participate in those systems I named? How can you speak their name when they're not around and share their career goals with influencers? How can you pay it forward to give people with fewer advantages than you a leg up? They might not have as many unearned advantages as you have.

Individuals can be antiracist by simply shopping at Black-owned businesses. By speaking up as an ally (more on this in Chapter 12).

By centering and amplifying Black voices. By listening to podcasts by Black podcasters and consuming content by Black creators.

It's not about you.

Give them those advantages and those opportunities that perhaps someone gave to you. It really does make a difference.

These actions that I'm talking about cost nothing. It's just goodwill. It's being a good ally.

It costs nothing to recommend someone who has fewer advantages than you for stretch assignments.

It costs nothing to give them credit.

It costs nothing to share their career goals with the right people.

You have more influence and control that you realize. Use the suggestions in this section to lift up other marginalized groups as well—not just Black folks. We all have something to give.

Inclusive 360 Action Steps

☐ Ensure the executive team is all on the same page with regards to responding to racial and social justice incidents.

☐ Hold listening sessions between Black employees and leadership, facilitated by a third party.

☐ Check in on your BRG leaders and provide them with extra support.

☐ Equip managers to hold these conversations with employees.

☐ Examine your products, systems, and marketing for racism.

Keep learning:

- Book: Me and White Supremacy by Layla F. Saad
- Book: How to Be an Antiracist by Ibram X. Kendi
- Film: 13th by Ava DuVernay (Netflix)
- Newsletter: Anti-Racism Daily www.antiracismdaily.com

WITH HOW THINGS are now, there will be more police violence and police killing of Black people like George Floyd and Breonna Taylor. There will be more calls for accountability. The next time that happens, will you stand up for your Black, Asian, Latinx, or other affected employees and go beyond words to change the systems and truly build an antiracist organization?

CHAPTER 8

R-E-S-P-E-C-T
Equitable Pay

Define pay equity

IN THE UNITED STATES, women on average earn 82 cents on the dollar to men. That's for all women.

- Asian-American women earn 90 cents on the dollar.
- White women earn 82 cents on the dollar.
- Black women earn 62 cents on the dollar.
- Native American women earn 57 cents on the dollar.
- Latina women earn 54 cents on the dollar.
- Mothers earn 70 cents on the dollar.[107]

Black and Latino men don't have it much better. Black men earn 87 cents on the dollar and Latinos earn 91 cents on the dollar compared to their white male peers. [108]

Additionally, at the age of 37, women's salaries drop to 67% of men's.

As a result of this pay gap, working women are estimated to miss out on $500 billion a year, according to a report from the American Association of University Women. [109]

Additionally, according to the World Economic Forum, unless things dramatically change, women will not hit pay equity with men until the year 2277. The report ranked 153 countries on how equitably men and women are paid. Iceland, a country with a federal law requiring equal pay, was number one. The United States was number 53.[110]

How did we get here? The short answer is: bias. Bias, in many forms. This includes employment discrimination (which could be unconscious bias), lack of pay transparency, lack of affordable childcare, and many more inequities that specifically affect marginalized people.

One subtle way pay has stayed inequitable is the common hiring practice of asking for salary history. The hiring practice of paying someone based on their previous salary perpetuates a cycle of women and underrepresented folks being underpaid. Low wages typically follow people from job to job, and this disproportionately affects women.

As of publication, almost 30 U.S. states now have laws that prohibit employers from requiring salary history from candidates. These laws attempt to break the cycle of underrepresented folks being underpaid. [111]

Another reason for the pay gap is that men are more likely to negotiate their salary. Women and other marginalized groups may not feel equipped to negotiate salary, either while negotiating their original contract, or as they move up in the organization. A study by Ranstadt Staffing found that 60% of women have never negotiated their salary, but 72% are willing to switch jobs for higher pay elsewhere.[112]

Hasbro created Ms. Monopoly to raise awareness of the gender pay gap. This is the first time in Monopoly history that there's a new mascot on the game's cover—a woman. In this version of the game, female players start with more money than male players and collect $240 Monopoly money when they pass GO, as opposed to men collecting $200. Players will still pull chance cards, go to jail, and pay taxes.

Instead of buying real estate, players will invest in inventions created by women. They can invest in things like Wi-Fi and chocolate chip cookies. The point is to start a conversation about the pay disparity between genders as well as raise awareness by giving female players the advantage for once.

According to a company statement, it's *"...a fun new take on the game that creates a world where women have an advantage often enjoyed by men. But don't worry, if men play their cards right, they can make more money too."*[113]

I bought the game, but my 10-year-old son won't play. It led to a great conversation about the pay gap, privilege, and the importance of being uncomfortable in order to learn and become more empathetic.

His favorite response when challenged like this is to say, "But I'm just a kid!" We talked through that, and ultimately, he understood. As someone who is surrounded by women (almost four moms, and four almost-stepsisters), he agrees the pay gap is unfair. But he still wasn't willing to get uncomfortable and play, to learn what it feels like to experience this inequity.

Can you blame him?

Get a scope of your pay disparities

As a result of these inequities and biases, most organizations have pay gaps, even if they're unintentional.

Salesforce has grown, in large part, through acquisitions. In acquiring other companies, Salesforce slowly began to realize that many of its acquisitions had a serious lack of pay parity. When Salesforce CEO Marc Benioff realized this in 2015, he quickly decided that the company would eliminate discrepancies in pay across gender. Since 2015, Salesforce has paid $12 million in pay discrepancies across gender, race, and ethnicity.

The possibilities are inspiring. On January 1, 2018, Iceland became the first country in the world to require equal pay, with a goal to eliminate the current 16% pay gap by 2022. The law requires that all companies and government agencies with 25 or more employees must have government certification of their equal-pay policies. Employers in violation of equal pay will face fines.

Leaders like Benioff and countries like Iceland see the win-win-win: employees feel more valued (and are paid equally); there's less turnover; and the company is ultimately more profitable. [114]

The ridesharing app Lyft, which has 4,600 salaried employees, achieved pay equity among male and female employees in the same job function.

Lyft began this process in 2016 by hiring an outside consultant to conduct an audit. According to the 2020 pay audit, Lyft says, *"We're happy to share that in 2020, we did not find any pattern of statistically significant pay disparities for different gender or racial groups after accounting for legitimate business factors like performance, experience, and location."*

This does not include drivers who are independent contractors.

"Hopefully, this is a wakeup call to others," Lyft board director Valerie Jarrett told *Forbes*.

Lyft was in pretty good shape already: the company found that less than 1% of its salaried workforce had differences in pay that couldn't be explained by legitimate business factors. The company then spent about $200,000 over a two-year period to adjust the salaries. [115]

The pay audit compared employees' base salaries and total compensation packages across gender in comparable roles.

The audit was less painful for Lyft than it was for Salesforce, in part, because of the way the companies have grown. *"It's a lot harder to change the culture once the company is up and running,"* Jarrett said. *"I am heartened that [founders] John Zimmer and Logan Green cared about this issue from Day 1."* [116]

Nordstrom achieved pay equity as well, and they have many more employees than Lyft: the company of 74,000 achieved pay equity on the basis of race and gender. The company evaluated pay equity by looking at base salary and analyzing it across similar gender, race, roles, levels of experience, and performance. [117]

Before starting your own pay equity journey, ensure you have executive level and legal counsel buy-in. Pay equity is a complex web of federal, state, and local laws that requires consulting legal counsel for guidance. You'll want to make sure you have support to correct any issues you find. You'll also want to make sure this is not a one-and-done practice. For growing organizations, I recommend a third-party pay equity audit at least once a year.

Another place pay disparity shows up is in prize money for events.

The Tim Hortons Brier and Scotties Tournament of Hearts is a major competition in the popular Canadian sport of curling and began to pay male and female teams equal prize money in 2020. This seems fairly obvious, but in the past, male players earned a $293,000 purse and female players earned a $165,000 purse. [118]

How can your organization follow the lead of these companies and create pay equity and equitable prize money? Follow the ARC.

ASK.

- What is the scope of your audit?
- What is the average pay for groups of people in the same job in the same location? Look at job title (department, location); pay data (base, bonus target, equity holdings); and finally, employee data (gender, race/ethnicity, age, highest education level, most recent performance evaluation score).
- Are there easy explanations for a disparity, such as performance evaluations? Look for any factor beyond gender that would explain the gaps you find.
- Are there gaps in pay equity that can be easily addressed?
- Are there policies that can be created to prevent wage gaps in the future? For example, if your firm merges with or acquires another, can you create a policy now that plans for pay equity after the merger?

RESPECT.

Respect the answers. Respect the data. Respect the respondents. Respect the process of accountability for following through on changes.

CONNECT.

Connect leaders' assessments to diversity and inclusion. Connect your employees to each other to hold open conversations about salary. Connect the answer to solutions. Solutions like this:

Create equitable hiring practices

Another part of your audit and corrections should be updating your hiring practices to ensure there is equity when new employees get hired. Establish a formal new employee compensation structure that eliminates negotiation and wages determined on a case-by-case basis.

When posting a job description, provide salary ranges. Providing salary ranges up front will show you're serious about making sure the talent you hire is treated equitably; you don't want to waste the candidate or the hiring manager's time; and will clearly define the experience level of the candidate you're looking for. The best candidates may not apply for a job unless the salary range is included.

The career website Hired.com virtually eliminated the gender gap in a study of 120,000 employees who found their job through Hired.com. The candidate profile form asks how much they want to get paid. That field used to be an empty box, and Hired.com found that women requested on average $4,000 less than comparable men.

Hired.com changed the form by pre-loading it with the median salary for a candidate's desired role, sending a message to women: "You're worth at least this!"

After the form was changed, the discrepancy disappeared. This was due to both women raising their asks and some men lowering theirs. The study of candidates from 6,700 companies was controlled for location, résumé characteristics, and experience.[119]

Get transparent with salaries

If salaries are leaked, it often creates office tension that can lead to decreased productivity and higher turnover. Going forward, consider making all employees' salaries public, as is the practice of many tech companies, with Buffer leading the way. Salary transparency can decrease pay and equity gaps—and help retain women and underrepresented talent.

For years, Buffer has publicly shared their salary formula, compensation philosophy, and the complete list of employee salaries on its website: https://buffer.com/salaries.

Full pay transparency is also the approach taken by the software company Unito, which created a salary matrix that lists salary by department, role, and seniority. The matrix also includes commission structures and company targets that could lead to salary increases.

Unito used salary and benefit compensation data from external sources to set average salaries for each specific role (according to skill set and level).

Candidates for open positions at Unito are told what their salary could be based on the figure in the matrix. There's no negotiating, as that tends to widen the pay gap because women and BIPOC are less likely to negotiate salary.

The company took it a step further—they increased the base salaries of roles typically dominated by women (like human resources) in non-management levels. This nearly 4% pay adjustment will compound, leading to an equitable amount of long-term earning potential, regardless of employee gender.[120]

Pay employees well

As of publication, the federal minimum wage of $7.25 per hour hasn't changed since 2009. [121] Some states and cities passed laws to set minimum wages higher than the federal minimum. For example, in Chicago where I live, the minimum wage is $15 per hour.[122] While it's great that some cities and states go above the minimum, the larger issue is that many people simply don't earn a living wage.

Hourly workers are disproportionally BIPOC. In fact, Black workers make up approximately 19% of essential jobs that pay less than $16.54 an hour, the wage necessary to meet the basic needs of a family of four.

The seemingly equitable solution is simply to pay your hourly workers more. While that may feel like a stretch for smaller businesses, many large companies are already doing it, and were doing so, even before the COVID-19 pandemic.

In 2020, many companies like Target and Walmart began paying their frontline workers more, at least during pandemic times, to recognize that these (often hourly) workers were literally putting themselves in a life-or-death situation by bagging groceries or ringing up a transaction. These and other companies made pay hikes permanent in 2021.[123]

In recent years, we've seen more companies begin to set increasingly higher base wages. In 2019, Fifth Third Bank increased its minimum wage to $18 per hour, a 200% increase from two years prior. The raise helped reduce employee turnover by 16% and affects almost 5,000 hourly employees.[124]

When considering the cost of hiring and onboarding employees, a 16% reduction in employee turnover is no joke. I'm quite sure many human resources leaders would be thrilled to reduce turnover by 16%.

Bank of America is another company doing the same. As of 2021, the bank's minimum wage is $20 per hour. This increases pay for 22,000 hourly employees.

"We are saying thank you, and sharing our success with our team-mates who serve our clients and communities every day," Sheri Bronstein, Bank of America's chief human resources officer, stated in a news statement.[125]

The reality is pretty simple: when people are paid well, respected, and appreciated, they tend to work harder and produce better results.

They're happier and it shows in their work and in their interactions with customers. The extra bonus compensation instills employee loyalty and helps retain employees and attract top talent.

In early 2020, pre-COVID-19, Delta Airlines gave all 90,000 employees bonuses that were the equivalent of two month's salary, or 16% of their annual salary. The profitable airline knows that re-investing in its employees leads to greater satisfaction, lower turnover, and happier customers.

Ed Bastian, CEO, said, *"For years, I would get beaten up by Wall Street. They thought the profits were theirs, and 'Why are you giving the profits away to the employees?'"* Bastian added, *"Wall Street has actually come full circle, and they realize that Delta is the most awarded airline in the world because of its employees."* [126]

Even smaller organizations can do this. St. John Properties, a real estate development company in Maryland achieved a major milestone. They then surprised all 198 employees with shares of a $10 million bonus. At their 2019 holiday party, each employee received a check averaging $50,000. [127]

Through an Employee Stock Ownership Program (ESOP), the clothing company Eileen Fisher is 60% owned by its namesake and 40% owned by employees (the majority of whom are women). [128]

Fisher told CNN, *"Once we started having extra profit, the first thought was to share it with the employees. They do all the work, it's only fair to share, which I think all companies should have to do. I really do. I think even 10% of the profits is good for morale and for people feeling like they're really a part of this company. People speak up more when they see things that don't feel right or if people are wasting money over there."*

Publix, the grocery chain in the Southeastern U.S., is the world's largest employee-owned company. After a year of work and 1,000 hours, employees are given company stock equal to roughly 8% to 12% of their annual compensation for free! They have the option to buy additional shares via a payroll deduction. The privately held company esti-mated that each share is worth $40.15, and it pays a quarterly dividend of roughly 22 cents per share.[129]

The result? A 5% employee churn rate in an industry with an average churn of 65%—that amounts to a massive savings in hiring and train-ing costs. Investing in your employees is an investment in your entire organization.

Inclusive 360 Action Steps

☐ Conduct a pay equity audit (or hire an outside firm to do so) and identify gaps and trends in your own organization.
☐ If necessary, update how your organization communicates pay information to potential candidates. If your current poli-cy requests salary history, stop doing so.
☐ Pay your hourly workers more!
☐ Look for opportunities to show your employees that they matter. Issue bonuses or consider an ESOP.

Keep learning:

- Book: The Memo by Minda Harts
- Game: Ms. Monopoly
- Game: Inequality-opoly

CHAPTER 9

Money, Money, Money

Equitable Spend and Access

Procure equitably

IN THE YEARS following the United States Civil Rights Act of 1964, President Nixon established the Office of Minority Business Enterprise. This required government agencies to contract with "minority-owned businesses." The private sector soon got on board with companies such as IBM and General Motors, launching similar programs.

Now thousands of organizations have **supplier diversity** programs or initiatives (typically housed in the procurement department) that expand access of corporate spending to traditionally underrepresented business owners. The goal is to create a supply chain that includes businesses certified by a third party such as the Women's Business Enterprise National Council, National Minority Supplier Development Council, United States Hispanic Chamber of Commerce, the National LGBT Chamber of Commerce, and the National Veteran Business Development Council.

These organizations certify businesses as majority women-owned, minority-owned, veteran-owned, Hispanic-owned, LGBTQ-owned, or otherwise owned by underrepresented Americans.

My own consulting firm is certified as both women-owned and LGBTQ-owned, and we leverage these certifications to get access to opportunities with larger organizations. Supplier diversity matters to small businesses like mine, because it provides access to significant spending power. Businesses owned by traditionally underrepresented people typically encounter more challenges (such as access to capital) than their counterparts. Supplier diversity provides a leg up.

Ultimately, the ripple effect to local communities is profound: these businesses can now create more jobs and generate more tax revenue.

Supplier diversity programs have real-world impact. CVS Health reported in 2018 that they spent $1 billion to diverse suppliers and ultimately contributed $5.5 billion to the U.S. economy and sustained 31,095 jobs. The company set a goal to increase their spending with diverse suppliers to $1.5 billion.[130]

A study by the Hackett Group found that companies with robust supplier diversity programs also have more cost-effective supply chains with a 33% return on the cost of operations. [131]

Supplier diversity matters so much that senior executives from leading companies gather twice a year at The Billion Dollar Roundtable. The Billion Dollar Roundtable was created in 2001 to convene corporations that achieved spending of at least $1 billion with minority and woman-owned suppliers. Members convene to review common issues, opportunities, and strategies. Being a part of the Billion Dollar Roundtable is prestigious, and member companies are recognized and celebrated for this achievement.

Marriott International now spends $500 million each year globally with women-owned businesses. This includes spending for both managed hotels and at corporate.

"Diversifying our global supply chain with people who represent a variety of communities and backgrounds is not only gratifying—it makes tremendous business sense," Ray Bennett, President of Marriott, said in a statement. *"Tapping a greater range of entrepreneurs spurs innovation, competition and ultimately business success."* [132]

You don't have to have a billion dollar procurement budget to set up informal supplier diversity programs within your own company. Start small to begin increasing your procurement spending with businesses owned by traditionally underrepresented people. Follow the ARC to get started.

ASK.

- Who are the suppliers with whom we spend the top 10% of our procurement budget? Are any of those businesses owned by members of underrepresented groups?
- Would other vendors qualify as a "diverse supplier?" This could be as simple as sending out an email survey to all suppliers and asking them to respond, or it could involve bringing in a third party to cross-reference your organization's suppliers with databases of certified companies.
- What are our current and upcoming procurement needs? Maybe you have an upcoming catered luncheon, need swag for an annual meeting, or are looking to do a brand refresh.

RESPECT

Respect the answers you find when you explore your procurement process. Actively listen to the numbers and the data—even if you don't like what it tells you. Especially if you don't like what it tells you. Don't dismiss what you find.

CONNECT

Connect these answers to solutions like proactively diversifying your supply chain. Connect solutions to accountability systems. Supplier diversity spending is easy to measure! It's a matter of dollars and cents.

Connect to solutions like:

Set a supplier diversity target.

What gets measured matters, so be sure to set clear targets when setting up your own version of a supplier diversity program. A great target is to work towards spending 30% of your procurement budget with diverse suppliers.

Identify diverse suppliers.

Reach out to the local chapters of certifying organizations and learn how you can connect with their member businesses. Examples include local chapters of the organizations I mentioned earlier: Women's Business Enterprise National Council, National Minority Supplier Development Council, United States Hispanic Chamber of Commerce, the National LGBT Chamber of Commerce, and the National Veteran Business Development Council.

Spend money with these businesses!

Whether it's through a formal Request for Proposal process, or through more informal channels, spend your procurement dollars with these businesses! Share the spend.

Supplier diversity is equity in action.

Set standards for your suppliers

Just as your organization can begin supplier diversity initiatives to support the business growth of underrepresented companies, you can also use your organization's buying power to influence companies not owned by underrepresented founders. Simply put, your organization's procurement spending can come with some strings attached.

SurveyMonkey, Eventbrite, Zoom, Intuit, 23andMe, and other tech companies joined together in a public commitment to require their partners and suppliers to invest in diversity, equity, and inclusion. These companies are using their buying power to demand systemic change.

The statement from Zander Lurie, CEO of SurveyMonkey, reads: *"We also want to help upend the system that has supported bias outside our walls. We are part of an ecosystem, a network of businesses that include our law firms, food suppliers, landlords, marketing agencies, and investment bankers. Collectively, we spend hundreds of millions of dollars with these organizations. Starting today, we will make sure we're spending our money with organizations that align with our values. I am looking forward to personally contacting our 20 largest vendors to inform them that investing in diversity, equity, and inclusion will be a requirement for doing business with us."*[133]

This matters because many organizations aren't motivated to commit to diversity, equity, and inclusion unless there's external pressure—like a requirement from a large client like SurveyMonkey. How can your organization use their leveraging and buying power to set DEI standards for your suppliers? You can actually use this SurveyMonkey template to send a message to your own suppliers: https://www.surveymonkey.com/mp/vendor-diversity-survey-template/.

Intel created an "Intel Rule" designed to increase diversity within the law firms they hire. As of 2021, they will only work with firms whose equity partners meet certain diversity thresholds.

Firms are eligible to do legal work for Intel only if they meet two diversity criteria: at least 21% of the firm's U.S. equity partners are women, and at least 10% of the firm's U.S. equity partners are under-represented people (which Intel specifically defines as equity partners whose race is other than full white/Caucasian, and partners who have self-identified as LGBTQ+, disabled, or as veterans).

Intel took a powerful stand in its press release: *"We understand that doing this may deny to us the services of many highly skilled lawyers, per-haps including the services of some law firms with which we have worked for decades. But Intel cannot abide the current state of progress—it is not enough, and progress is not happening fast enough. At Intel, below average and average on diversity is no longer good enough to be a member of our regular outside counsel roster."*[134]

In 2017, HP did something similar. They made it a contractual con-dition that its external law firm partners meet diversity criteria. They withheld partial payments until firms met the new diversity metrics, and 95% of their partner firms are now compliant. [135]

Coca-Cola's legal department provided similar tough guidelines for their outside law firms. They now require at least 30% of associate and partner work on new matters to be billed by underrepresented lawyers. Of that amount, at least half of the billable hours should go to Black lawyers. [136]

It's a powerful incentive when large businesses require their partners to be more diverse. I recommend that you hold your own suppliers ac-countable. Doing so creates opportunities for businesses owned by un-derrepresented groups—like my own.

Revisit donations and partnerships

Finally, organizations should pay attention to their partnerships and where they donate funds. For example, many organizations have received employee and public backlash after it has been released that they donate to political candidates who have a proven anti-LGBTQ track record.[137]

Other organizations received major criticism for supporting the National Rifle Association (NRA) after the association resisted calls for gun control legislation in the aftermath of various school massacres in the United States. Some, such as major airlines, hotels, and car rental agencies, simply ended discounts for NRA members. Others, like Charles Schwab, took away clients' ability to donate to NRA-affiliated charities through its donor-advised fund.[138]

If your organization or your organization's leaders are major donors, or public supporters of people or groups that are anti-equality, it may make good business sense to reconsider that support. Millennial and Generation Z employees and customers, in particular, prioritize organizations that support equality.[139]

Increase access to shelf space

Another area inequities show up is in the amount of shelf space afforded to white-owned businesses compared to that of BIPOC-owned businesses. Most companies that sell products primarily carry products from white-owned businesses, despite the fact that 13% of the United States population is Black. This lack of access to shelf-space continues racial inequities that contribute to the racial wealth gap.

If your organization sells products of any kind, who are the purveyors of those products?

In 2020, the 15 Percent Pledge was launched by Aurora James to encourage retailers to commit a minimum of 15 Percent of their shelf-space to Black-owned businesses. The 15 Percent is a 501c3 non-profit advocacy organization seeking economic equality and prosperity for Black future founders, Black students, and Black people in the workforce.

Major retailers like Sephora and Rent the Runway have already signed on. Artemis Patrick, Chief Merchandising Officer, Sephora wrote,*"We recognize we can do better and this pledge builds on our ongoing work to use our resources to drive meaningful and long-term change for Sephora and our industry."* [140]

Other companies to take the pledge include West Elm and Bloomingdale's.

Macy's is the largest retailer to join the 15 Percent Pledge and took their commitment a step further. The retailer launched five exclusive collections with Black fashion designers in 2021.

Although Lowe's has yet to sign the 15 Percent Pledge, the company created a small business pitch competition for underrepresented founders. Businesses can apply and receive mentorship from Lowe's and partner Daymond John. Up to 375 businesses can even earn shelf space at the store, creating great access and equity for underrepresented founders who may lack influential networks. [141]

In an effort to provide greater visibility to companies that are minority-owned, Giant Foods began labeling products on its shelves accordingly. More than 3,100 food and nonfood products feature the updated shelf labels across Giant's 164 stores. The products are produced by 281 minority-owned businesses. [142]

Target is doing something similar. Target's employee-led Black History Month initiative showcases 100+ products (that are carried all year long) that celebrate Black history, legacy, and culture. Many of these products are produced by Black-owned businesses.

The website now makes it easy to identity products from Black-owned businesses, which receive extra promotions during Black History Month.

This initiative began a few years ago as a program created by Target's African American Business Council, a business resource group (more on those in Chapter 10). The Council includes more than 1,000 employees who first created the assortment five years ago and continues to advise product teams on the collection. Now more than 100 products that are $29.99 or less are in the collection.

Target's Black Beyond Measure campaign tells stories not only of these businesses but of the company's Black employees. That's a stunning example of how you amplify underrepresented voices.[143]

Other retailers discovered they were having the opposite problem: not only were companies like Walgreens, CVS, and Walmart not spotlighting BIPOC-owned brands, they were actively preventing BIPOC customers from purchasing beauty products. For years, beauty and hair products for BIPOC people were locked up behind plexiglass and only accessible with employee assistance, whereas beauty and hair products for white customers were not!

It wasn't until 2020 that the three retailers stopping displaying these products behind locked cases.[144]

Invest in underrepresented founders

In a study of U.S. venture activity from 2015–2019, just 2.4% of Venture Capital-backed entrepreneurs were BIPOC. In 2020, the percentage increased incrementally, with 2.6% of BIPOC entrepreneurs getting funding.[145]

Based on data from the Brookings Institution, less than a third (29%) of Black-owned small businesses and only half (50%) of Latinx-owned small businesses that apply for business loans from large banks receive approval. That number jumps to 60% for white small business applicants. [146]

Is this because BIPOC entrepreneurs are less creative? Less innovative?

No, in most cases, they simply don't have access to the decision-makers. They don't typically have the same professional networks that come from prestigious colleges and generational wealth. Because of bias and a lack of network connections, these businesses are dramatically under-funded by investors, furthering the racial equity gap. However, there are major businesses that have taken this into their own hands and are directly investing in underrepresented businesses.

Sephora Beauty's Accelerate Incubation program is one such program designed to provide greater access. In 2020, the program shifted to exclusively support BIPOC-owned beauty businesses. The program gives opportunity and exposure to businesses typically under-resourced.

This is especially notable because Sephora came under fire in 2019 for racially profiling customers and had closed stores for anti-bias training. This Accelerate program is one of many new antiracist initiatives launched by Sephora.

Accelerate is a six-month intensive boot camp created to teach the required skills to build a successful business. The program includes training, mentorship, lessons on grants and funding, and more. The goal is to eventually launch these products at Sephora. [147]

The bra company Third Love created a similar program, the TL Effect, designed to support BIPOC-founders who own consumer-facing brands. This program provides financial, professional, and marketing support with a larger goal to ultimately increase the number of Black women CEOs in Fortune 500 companies. [148]

In the beverage and alcohol space (and adjacent products), Constellation Brands Ventures committed to investing $100 million in Black and minority-owned businesses over the next 10 years. They're also providing pro-bono sales, marketing, and operations expertise to support the success of those businesses. [149]

Constellation Brands Ventures had great success with its similar Focus on Female Founders Initiative, which increased the firm's portfolio of businesses from 20% female-owned to 50% female-owned.

Target has a similar initiative, committing millions of dollars and up to 10,000 hours of pro bono consulting to BIPOC-owned businesses in Minneapolis and St. Paul, Minnesota, where the company is based. [150]

Netflix is taking it a step further, having already moved $25 million in their investments to lenders that serve the Black community. The company committed to moving 2% of its cash on hand, or up to $100 million, to institutions such as the Hope Credit Union, which is a Black-owned bank. The Hope Credit Union serves 1.5 million Black Americans but doesn't have the resources to fully address their customer's needs. [151]

Even if your organization is small, what resources does it have to pay it forward? How can it deeply support marginalized communities through its spending, investments, donations, and even by paying employees to provide pro-bono support to community organizations or diverse suppliers?

Inclusive 360 Action Steps

☐ Examine your existing suppliers and survey to see how many are already owned by underrepresented individuals and/or certified as such.

☐ Partner with local certifying organizations.

☐ Who are your top three vendors? What kinds of DEI benchmarks can you ask them to achieve?

☐ Scrutinize the partnerships your organization has and suspend donations and partnerships to those who do not share your organization's values.

☐ Ensure at least 15% of your shelf space is dedicated to products made by Black-owned businesses. Dedicate additional shelf space to other underrepresented groups.

☐ Choose at least one additional way for your organization to invest in marginalized communities.

Keep learning:

- Book: Hacking Supplier Diversity by Scott Vowels
- Book: It's About Damn Time by Arlan Hamilton
- 15 Percent Pledge: www.15percentpledge.org

Part 3:
INCLUSION

CHAPTER 10

Come Together
Understanding Inclusion

Ask your employees

DIVERSITY, WHILE IMPORTANT, means nothing without giving those underrepresented folks a valuable voice in the workplace—without making those diverse voices feel included. In this section, I'll explore numerous approaches to creating an inclusive workplace, but they all must have strong buy-in from leadership.

Inclusion requires a big picture, 360 degree approach to each business unit and department of your organization. Every business unit and every department needs inclusive systems. Inclusion must be built into product and service design, product marketing, and the employee experience. You run the risk of hypocrisy or accusations of box-checking if you don't take a comprehensive approach.

Look at the organization from all angles by once again using the ARC Method*:

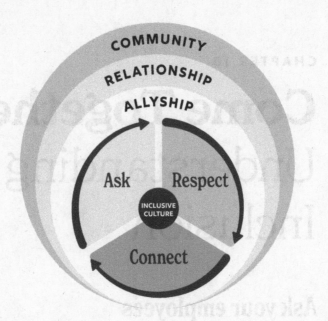

ASK.

Ask questions such as:

- Who else needs to be part of this conversation?
- Are our products and services inclusive?
- Is the marketing of our products and services inclusive?
- Do we provide the same benefits to our customer facing employees that we provide our salaried employees?
- Do we have equal benefits for LGBTQ+ and non-LGBTQ+ employees?
- Do our policies exclude anyone?

RESPECT.

Respect the answers you find when you ask questions like those above. Actively listen to the numbers and the data—even if you don't like what it tells you. Especially if you don't like what it tells you. Don't dismiss what you find.

CONNECT.

Connect these answers to solutions. Connect solutions to accountability systems. And connect the accountability for solutions to leaders' assessments, so leaders are more invested in the change.

DEI initiatives are not sustainable unless systems and behavior change. But of course, you can't know what systems need change unless you carefully assess the systems. Start by getting key stakeholders on board to conduct a robust employee inclusion survey. Bring together any formal or informal DEI leads, Head of HR, CEOs for smaller organizations, or anyone other relevant parties, to map out the survey process, including how you'll share and use the results. If you have a DEI Council, they should take the lead on this initiative.

Follow the ARC Method® when preparing, conducting, and debriefing your inclusion survey. The consulting company Paradigm created an inclusion survey with SurveyMonkey that's a great place to start: https://www.surveymonkey.com/r/belonging_inclusion_template.

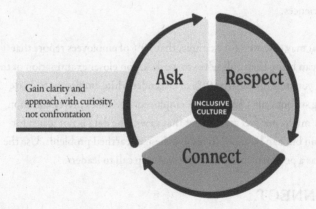

ASK.

Here are some of the questions you can Ask in the survey, which are on a strongly agree to strongly disagree scale:

- I feel like I belong at my organization.

- I can voice a contrary opinion without fear of negative consequences.
- When I speak up at work, my opinion is valued.
- I feel respected and valued by my teammates in my organization.
- I feel respected and valued by my manager in my organization.

In your promotion of the survey, provide a brief overview of its purpose (and why each response matters), a clear deadline (1–2 weeks), and a reassurance of anonymity. Be extra clear about privacy and anonymity to maximize the responses from underrepresented folks who may not otherwise feel safe to complete the survey.

RESPECT.

Take the time to carefully respect and process the results, even those that may be ugly and disheartening, even those that bruise some egos. Pay special attention to differences among demographics. The most insightful data may come when you examine differences in employee experiences.

You may discover, for example, that 79% of employees report that they can bring their full selves to work. Upon closer examination of the data, you may realize that 91% of cisgender white employees feel safe doing so, but only 65% of Black employees do. That's pretty common, but it might not feel great to get that news. The data is not just information but can be a tool to resolve these unearthed problems. Use the data as a powerful and persuasive wake-up call to leaders.

CONNECT.

So, what are you going to do about what you learned? And how are you going to communicate it?

As you communicate the survey results throughout the organization, please don't share all the data! That can lead to overwhelm, distraction, excuses, and inaction. It's more than enough to share some of the higher-level insights and resulting goals and objectives. Make sure you communicate that the data matters and you have a plan of action.

As you review the survey results, consider the following:

- What is the most common theme in these problems?
- Which of these problems, if any, can be solved with a quick fix?
- Which of these problems, if solved, can most meaningfully impact the employee experience?

The best process is to rinse and repeat. Repeat the survey every 6–12 months, track progress (or lack of), and take new action. Always connect the results to real solutions.

This section is full of specific solutions such as:

Develop Business Resource Groups

Does your organization have an Employee Resource Group (ERG) or Business Resource Group (BRG)? These terms are frequently used interchangeably, although I'll use BRG in this book. Other terms you might see used are affinity groups, community groups, and network groups.

These are organization-sponsored groups of employees typically organized around a demographic. BRGs are typically one of the first inclusion initiatives that an organization chooses because they're relatively easy to set up and are often employee-driven.

Here are some of the most popular types of BRGs:

- Caregiver (dual earner parents, single parents, adoptive parents, elder caregivers, health-related, disability, etc.)
- Cultural diversity and/or geographic area
- Flexible/Remote workers

- Generations
- LGBTQ+ employees
- Men and dads at the workplace
- People with disabilities
- Religious affiliations
- Veterans
- Women in the workplace

Xerox is known for having the first BRG, the National Black Employee Caucus, formed in 1970, followed by the Black Women's Leadership Caucus, formed in 1980. Hewlett Packard is recognized for forming the first LGBTQ+ BRG in 1978. [152]

BRGs have long been important spaces for employees to connect with one another and find their voice and sense of belonging in the workplace. More recently, BRGs have been increasingly asked to support the organization's business goals and diversity and inclusion strategies. I believe BRGs should always have a business imperative, which can lead to them being more highly valued by organizational leadership.

Here are some great ways organizations can utilize their BRG to further their broader diversity, equity, and inclusion initiatives:

- Ask for feedback on culturally appropriate and sensitive product development and/or marketing.
- Ask for advice on where to look for underrepresented talent, more awesome people like themselves.
- Ask for advice on better engaging their underrepresented talent.
- Ask for feedback on specific business development opportunities.
- Ask for suggestions on diverse suppliers for procurement
- Invite members to sit on panel discussions.
- Promote your organization to the larger community as a great place to work.

Here are some ways organizations should NOT use their BRG:

- You should not use your BRG members as unpaid trainers doing the emotional labor of educating others about their own community.
- You should not take photos of your BRG members for internal communications to show that you value diversity if you're not doing any of the other work towards inclusion.

BRGs only work if both the employees and the organization feel invested in the group's success. It's critical for every BRG to have an Executive Sponsor (a senior leader willing to be an ally) who advocates for the group at senior levels.

Here are some great ways to set the BRG up for success:

- Allow BRG leaders to dedicate a certain percentage or number of working hours directly to the BRG.
- Publicly acknowledge the contributions and accomplishments of BRG leaders and members in internal communications throughout the organization.
- Ensure BRG leaders are compensated for their leadership, or at least receive a more significant professional development stipend.
- Engage senior leaders in the work of the BRG to not only build relationships with members but also identify promising sponsees (more on sponsorship programs in Chapter 9).

Some BRGs start "grassroots-style"—from the employee up, and some are started by leadership. When you're ready to start, follow the ARC:

ASK.

- Who will benefit from a BRG? Why?
- How would a BRG support the organization's mission, vision, and values?
- How would it support the organization's other DEI initiatives?

RESPECT.

Respect the differing perspectives you'll hear when asking these hard questions. Don't dismiss anyone's point of view.

CONNECT.

Connect these answers to solutions—like actually starting the BRG!

BRGs could focus on a million different things: educating allies, celebrating cultural traditions, specific business imperatives, engaging with community-based nonprofit organizations, and so on. Make sure that your organization's vision for the BRG, and the BRG's own vision, align. If the senior leaders envision the BRG as an educational and ally-building tool, but the group envisions itself as focusing on social justice, then there could be a serious misalignment that could lead to challenges later.

Whirlpool's LGBTQ+ PRIDE BRG was one such group that had a social justice focus. In 2018, a bill was introduced in the city of St. Joseph, Michigan, to add sexual orientation and gender identity to the city's anti-discrimination policy. Around that time, a lesbian employee of Whirlpool Headquarters in St. Joseph, Michigan, told her manager that she was afraid of putting a photo of her partner on her desk, out of fear of her partner losing her job (at a company that didn't protect LGBTQ+ employees).

The manager realized that although Whirlpool had an LGBTQ+ inclusive anti-discrimination policy, that wasn't the case everywhere, and it certainly wasn't the case in Michigan. The concerned manager spoke with other leaders at the company and the company agreed to fully support the proposed anti-discrimination ordinance in St. Joseph. Whirlpool wanted to make sure that, beyond the walls of their organization, employees felt safe to be openly LGBTQ+.

The company's PRIDE BRG built a coalition of local and Michigan-wide LGBTQ+ organizations to advocate for this public policy change in St. Joseph. They provided LGBTQ+ education for company employees and the community at large and spoke at public hearings. With the support of Whirlpool and the coalition, St. Joseph became the first community in the tri-county area—and one of only 45 in Michigan—to enact an ordinance protecting LGBTQ+ residents from discrimination. [153]

BRGs can have an incredible impact, but a common challenge I hear from BRG leaders is keeping members involved. Everyone has competing priorities, both in their job role and in their personal lives. It can be challenging to keep members engaged, especially when people are working remotely. A simple way to engage members is to survey them and ask them to rank their priorities and needs from the group.

No matter where your organization is in the BRG development journey, it's critical to keep checking in and following the ARC Method®:

ASK.

- Ask members, "What do you need?"
- Ask for their advice on business objectives.
- Ask what their goals are for the BRG.
- Ask what the demographics are of the BRG. What about the demographics of leadership?
- Ask what it means to be a great ally to each group.
- Ask if employees throughout the organization, and throughout its various offices, are represented in the BRG, not just people in the main corporate office.
- Ask members if they feel valued by leadership.
- Ask BRG leadership about the level of engagement with remote workers.

RESPECT.

Thoughtfully listen to those who are brave enough to share their stories. Respect the answers and stories you find when you ask questions like those above. Actively listen to the numbers and the data—even if you don't like what it tells you. Especially if you don't like what it tells you. Don't dismiss what you find.

CONNECT.

Connect these answers to solutions. Connect solutions to accountability systems. For example, measure whether BRG leaders or members are increasingly likely to get promoted. Hold executive sponsors accountable for their BRG's success so those leaders are more invested in the group.

Connect your employees to each other to hold open conversations through listening sessions and informal chats during virtual meetings.

You'll quickly realize that BRGs will receive more support from leadership if you share concrete data that illustrate its impact. Combine an annual member survey with data such as the number of attendees at events, number of members involved in leadership, and the number of events you've hosted, and you'll get a good picture of the BRG's impact.

Once you have a sense of your members' interests and the organization's business objectives or expectations from the BRG, use the ARC Method® to prioritize goals.

ASK.

These are some of the questions we Ask to help BRGs prioritize:

- Which of these ideas can be quick wins?
- Which of these ideas will have a direct impact on the organization's business goals?
- Which of these ideas requires support from external departments?

RESPECT.

Respect the answers. Respect the data. Stay true.

CONNECT.

Connect the answers to specific solutions and goals. Connect those solutions and goals to systems of accountability (through committees or BRG leadership).

Increasingly, organizations are investing in BRG members and leaders through identity-specific leadership development programming, and cross-BRG events. Women's, Black, LGBTQ+ and other leadership summits are common particularly within larger organizations.

BRGs can certainly be siloed, focusing solely on their own interest areas. Within an organization, however, various BRGs may share similar challenges, similar concerns, and similar priorities. They may find incredible power in collaborating to leverage their collective concerns towards more meaningful action. A best practice is for organizations to have quarterly cross-BRG leader meetings or retreats.

The murder of George Floyd by a Minneapolis police officer on May 30, 2020 was a catalyst for organizations to embrace intersectionality. You may remember intersectionality refers to the additional challenges faced by people with multiple marginalized identities.

emPOWERing BRG Members

A major international auditing firm recognized that many of their employees were struggling to show up authentically at work and facing difficulties as they were promoted. Although the firm had done traditional leadership training before, they hadn't done it within the lens of inclusivity, authenticity, and self-empowerment. Together with an external executive coach, Heather Vickery from Vickery and Co., they developed a series of interactive webinars and group coaching sessions, collectively called emPOWERment.

emPOWERment began within the LGBTQ+ BRG. Throughout the sessions, Vickery worked with emissaries on the skills necessary to expand business connections, increase client connectivity/engagement and create accountability systems to be more effective.

After a successful first cohort with 20 members of the Pride BRG, emPOWERment was opened up to the other BRGs as well. Anyone in the firm can be nominated, and emPOWERment has become the firm's top leadership coaching experience.

Through the emPOWERment program, these emerging leaders develop a stronger sense of purpose and begin stepping up more eagerly, which allows them to meet goals, create accountability and have more successful internal development. This "whole employee" approach helps emissaries achieve a more impactful, authentic, and empowering experience both in and out of the office.

George Floyd's murder happened just before Pride month (which was largely celebrated virtually due to COVID-19). And, as a result of the increasing dialogue around racial equity, we saw many organizations' Pride BRGs collaborate with Black BRGs on programming related to the Black LGBTQ+ experience.

In preparation for the workshops I personally led during June 2020, I had meetings with the leaders of both the Black and LGBTQ+ BRGs to ensure my teaching content reflected the diversity of the communities. I'm happy to say that it does, and I'm grateful to be checked on that! I'm grateful that these conversations are happening.

BRGs are a great place to look for engaged employees. These are the employees who are eager to learn and grow, even if they're allied group members.

But BRGs are just one of many great ways to ensure your organization can fulfill its promise to underrepresented employees. In the next few chapters, I'll share more great ideas to build a more inclusive organization, but it must start with establishing a baseline—it must start with asking great questions.

Inclusive 360 Action Steps

☐ Conduct an employee inclusion survey.
☐ Give your employees permission to start a Business Resource Group and provide full support and executive sponsorship.
☐ Empower any BRGs you do have by providing additional professional development opportunities.
☐ Create spaces for cross-BRG collaboration.

Keep learning:

- Podcast: Next Pivot Point
- Software: ERG Insight: www.cockerhamassociates.com
- Catalyst: www.catalyst.org/topics/ergs

CHAPTER 11

Just the Way You Are

Inclusive Conversations

IN THE AFTERMATH of the 2020 election in the United States, when tensions were running high, Dr. Natalie J. Hallinger posted the following on LinkedIn:

> *"As a behavioral scientist, I absolutely have to admit this—despite my personal feelings on the matter, but the folks suggesting that US #Democrats reach out to sympathize with and/or understand supporters of 45 are absolutely *right*.*
>
> *You don't achieve deep or lasting #behaviorchange through shame and ridicule.*
>
> *Hear me out.*
>
> *Whether your goal is*
> *+ interrogation*
> *+ cult deprogramming*
> *+ recruitment*
> *+ team cohesion*
> *+ weight loss*

+ climate protection
+ vaccine acceptance
+ any other behavior change

The way to successfully convince someone/anyone to
   - listen to you
   - respect you
   - care about you
   - agree with you
   - behave like you

necessarily includes making that person feel listened to, cared about, and respected, first.

The task may not be desirable, it's just how humans work."[154]

That's behavior change 101, and you'll find some great approaches in this section of the book.

Use your story

Maya Angelou famously said, *"I've learned that people will forget what you said, people will forget what you did, but people will never forget how you made them feel."* [155]

Humans change when they feel the need to change, not when someone is forcing them to change. I'm sure you can think of some examples of that within our own life. Feeling the need requires emotional triggers. And emotions are often triggered by stories. Look at any television episode or movie that made you cry—chances are, it had a compelling story that triggered your emotion. Have you ever seen the television show, "This Is Us?" I swear, every episode is specifically written and performed to make us cry!

The most obvious emotional trigger for behavior change is empathy, or taking the perspective of someone else. Taking the perspective of someone else can help us become more compassionate and better problem solvers.

Another very powerful emotion for behavior change is embarrassment or shame. Chances are, if someone has embarrassed themselves, or put their foot in their mouth in front of a client or colleague, they won't make that mistake again. Remember my story about the time I assumed someone was pregnant, and I learned the hard way that she wasn't? I was so embarrassed. But now I know better than to make that kind of an assumption.

Other powerful emotions include the feeling of being left out/ excluded, the feeling of being dismissed, and the feeling of being condescended to. All of these emotions can be used to create behavior change.

Many of us can probably think back to a manager or co-worker who triggered those feelings at least once, although I hope I'm wrong. Chances are, you won't ever forget the way you felt during that experience. That experience may have changed the way that you interact with that manager and/or people around you. Whether that's for better or worse.

So, how do we trigger emotions such as empathy, embarrassment, exclusion, dismissal, and condescension in order to change behavior?

Stories.

Emotions are triggered by storytelling.

When I'm leading a training, I make sure it's full of stories with hooks that can get buy-in and engagement from the audience. You'll find the most powerful speakers and trainers do exactly the same thing. And those stories don't have to be personal experiences—they can be stories ripped from the headlines. You don't have to hire a speaker or trainer to tell the stories that lead to buy-in and investment in DEI. There are great stories all around your workplace.

Start with yourself. In your past work experience, did you ever have a co-worker or manager who caused you to feel excluded, dismissed, or condescended to? Have you ever put your foot in your mouth in front of a colleague or client? Have you ever kept a personal matter a secret at work because you didn't want to over-share?

There's always a story. Those stories become unforgettable because they sting.

Your stories matter, and so do those of everyone around you. How do your colleagues feel about their experience within the organization?

A few years ago, I worked with a client on an eLearning project that used storytelling to build empathy around microaggressions and unconscious bias. My team created an anonymous survey and asked questions such as, "Have you ever had bias directed at you by another employee?" and "Have you ever witnessed bias by one employee towards another employee?"

We distributed the survey to the various Business Resource Groups and received some powerful, anonymous stories of micro- and macro-aggressions that then informed our eLearning project. The project included employee stories as told by actors.

Other ways you can collect great stories are during employee listening sessions/Courageous Conversations and exit interviews: "How inclusive do you think our organization is for employees of different backgrounds and perspectives?"

Of course, you risk not getting an honest answer, but it's nonetheless a great question to ask.

The combination of data and storytelling can change behavior because it appeals to both the heart and the mind. To successfully get buy-in at every stage of your DEI journey, you must thoughtfully present both arguments.

Minimize covering

In its 2013 study, Uncovering Talent, Deloitte explained why true inclusion is elusive:

> *"The ideal of inclusion has long been to allow individuals to bring their authentic selves to work. However, most inclusion efforts have not explicitly and rigorously addressed the pressure to conform that prevents individuals from realizing that ideal."*[156]

That pressure to conform leads to **"covering"**—or hiding parts of ourselves to avoid stigmatization. You may have also heard the term **"code-switching"**—those terms are often used interchangeably. It's incredibly difficult to create an inclusive culture when covering is persistent.

Deloitte found that an astounding 61% of workers cover parts of themselves at work, including 45% of straight white men.

People may hide elements that could draw unwanted attention to their race, religion, health, parental status, political party, and so forth. And when people can't fully be themselves at work, they under-perform.

Here are some common examples of covering:

- Staying in the closet as a member of the LGBTQ+ community
- Speaking less "Black" in the workplace
- Staying silent about a personal or family illness or disability
- Downplaying any religious affiliation
- Hiding a lack of college education
- A woman not speaking about being a parent so others don't assume she's not fully committed to work

A while ago I went through an unexpected and painful divorce. Many of my work colleagues had met my wife at various events, and for many of them, we were the first lesbian couple they knew to get married and later have a kid. I put a lot of pressure on myself to role model the white picket fence fantasy. People were cheering for us.

When I was in the middle of my separation and divorce, I didn't tell anyone in my work life. When clients and work colleagues asked about my wife, I'd answer evasively or tell white lies. I was distracted and unfocused, even with clients. I wasn't as proactive as I could have been.

I was ashamed. I felt that if people knew the truth about my marriage ending, they'd be disappointed in me. I'd somehow let them down.

Of course, in the rear-view mirror, I can see that the pressure to be the perfect lesbian couple came from me and no one else. When my work colleagues eventually found out, they were kind and supportive. I had put up walls for no good reason. I realize now that we were just another couple getting divorced, and our gender made no difference.

During that time in my life, I was covering. Everyone does at some point.

But it affects our work.

How do we create a workplace where the pressure to cover is minimized, where people can truly feel like they belong and can bring their full selves to work? Those workplaces are psychologically safe.

Build psychologically safe teams

Truly inclusive work cultures have **psychological safety**. Psychological safety is a term defined by Harvard Business School Professor Amy Edmonson as the *"belief that one will not be punished or humiliated for speaking up with ideas, questions, concerns or mistakes."*

At work, psychologically safe people don't feel pressure to conform, downplay any part of their identity, or hide significant personal problems. They don't feel pressure to cover. And if they feel psychologically safe enough to be their full selves, chances are, they also feel safe enough to share their biggest, boldest, and most innovative ideas.[157]

Google conducted a two-year internal study and found that the number one indicator of their top 180 high-performing teams was psychological safety. The people in these teams don't fear rejection from their team. They feel safe enough to take interpersonal risks and are able to bring themselves fully to work. [158]

You can start small to create psychological safety. One health care organization asks employees to smile and greet anyone who comes within 10 feet of them. That's a small, actionable habit that creates a welcoming environment at work.

A more significant way to create psychological safety is for leaders to demonstrate this themselves, to show genuine emotion and be vulnerable enough to admit failure, talk about their own fears, concerns, and areas to improve.

During the early days of COVID-19, I led a Zoom meeting during which a leader asked for tools to support the nearly 3,000 employees recently laid off by his company. I routinely woke up to email announcements and LinkedIn posts about more furloughs. I spoke with many clients struggling to support their Black employees after the murder of George Floyd.

And there's more. So much more. I'm sure you have a story or two of your own difficult decisions and struggles during COVID-19 and beyond. There's a lot of extra stress these days, and leaders feel it, too.

It's completely OK to not have all the answers. Or all of the resources. Or all of the self-care tools. Or the capacity to give to your many competing priorities. If you are able, it's OK to call it a day, sit on the couch, eat some pretzels, and watch reality TV.

Leaders have feelings, too. Perhaps you'll consider talking about yours. Now is not the time for leaders to "cover" themselves. It is a time to double-down on authenticity.

Share your own vulnerability, which as Dr. Brené Brown revealed, is a strength, not a weakness. This could mean that you share a story about a time you struggled to maintain balance, or a time you felt like an outsider, or maybe about what it was like when you started at the company.

Why?

Because it creates psychological safety. Your vulnerability gives your team permission to do the same: to share more of their own feelings and concerns. When leaders are vulnerable, it can create psychological safety among team members.

If you open up, talk about your feelings, and give your team permission to do the same, you have the chance to build greater trust on your team. This can be incredibly transformative for your organization—and sustainable as long as the behavior continues long after the pandemic. Chances are, you'll probably also see more of your team members stick around, too.

Vulnerability must be followed up with curiosity—genuine curiosity about what's going on with each individual on your team. Show an interest in each individual—in their personal background, their goals, their challenges, and their vision for the organization. You can demonstrate curiosity by following the ARC Method*. There are specific questions at the end of this chapter.

For leaders making the difficult decisions, this is the time to speak up more than ever. Do not hide. One of my closest friends trusted her leader immensely—but when my friend was among the many laid off, the leader disappeared, not even responding to kind words from their team. There was no empathy, no gratitude, no acknowledgment—only absence. I suppose that leader needed to recharge. Fair enough.

But recharging eventually becomes hiding, and my friend felt hurt and betrayed.

DELTA CEO ED BASTIAN modeled psychologically safe leadership when he spoke about his approach to connecting with his Black employees, *"If those individuals are not coming to you, you need to go find them because they exist within your organizations. And you need to make it safe. It takes time. It takes courage... And you don't have the answers, by definition, because you're born of privilege and you don't understand and appreciate that. So coming at it from a humble heart in really seeking to learn and understand is so powerful. There's no company out there of any size that doesn't have these stories within its four walls. And it's a journey. I'm still learning. I'm beginning to appreciate and I feel empowered to be their advocate and their ally. But I still need to understand what that means because I want to be a great advocate for them. You need to keep those conversations moving. You need to give people the permission to tell you when your ideas aren't good or you're not being responsive or as aware as you need. And I've given all of our, particularly our Black employees, that permission."* [159]

How will you make your team feel? Your own vulnerability is a gift you can give others—and you may be surprised by how it also opens you up to receive.

Train all leaders and managers

As your organization grows to include more underrepresented talent, it's critical to ensure all managers and leaders attend inclusive leader trainings.

An inclusive leader training addresses the unconscious bias that shows up in leadership and management decisions. For example, in

Chapter 2, I addressed the different types of bias that shows up in hiring decisions. And in Chapter 4, I wrote about the bias that shows up in performance assessments. An inclusive leader training provides tools and strategies to mitigate those biases.

This training also reminds leaders that it's so important to give appropriate credit and speak the name of underrepresented employees. So often the contributions of women and BIPOC have been overlooked, overshadowed, or decentered. Inclusive leaders speak those names.

A great example of this goes to Dr. Anthony Fauci. In speaking about the COVID-19 vaccine, he specifically said, *"The first thing you might want to say to my African American brothers and sisters is that the vaccine that you're going to be taking was developed by an African American woman."* [160]

He was deliberate to give Dr. Kizzy Corbett credit. To specifically amplify her. She earned it, and Dr. Fauci used his privilege to say her name. That's an example of inclusive leadership.

Inclusive leader training also shares actionable ways to help leaders build psychologically safe teams through curiosity, vulnerability, and humility. In my firm's inclusive leader training, we take leaders through the ARC Method* as a way to connect with employees during one-on-one meetings:

In this context, let's say that Taylor, who has recently joined your team, seems closed off and possibly overwhelmed.

Let's take this situation through the ARC. Again, as with the other ARC examples, context and tone matter! Approach with curiosity, not confrontation!

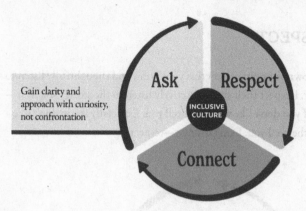

Gain clarity and approach with curiosity, not confrontation

ASK.

In this situation, you are asking questions of Taylor during your one-on-one. Here are some sample ways to ask for more clarity:

- What do you perceive we could be doing differently that could allow you to reach your goals and perform at a higher level?
- What do you look forward to when you come back each day?
- What would you change about your job?
- What would make your job more satisfying?
- What talents would you like to use in your current role?
- What can I do to best support you?
- Are you feeling seen and supported as an individual?

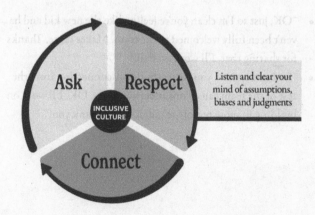

Listen and clear your mind of assumptions, biases and judgments

RESPECT.

Put down your phone, uncross your arms, and thoughtfully listen to Taylor. Respect their stories. Actively listen to the stories you hear— even if you don't like what they tell you. Especially if you don't like what they tell you. Don't dismiss—respect.

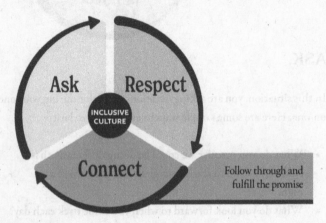

CONNECT.

In this context, connect is about paraphrasing and validating. Here are some conversation starters or ways that you can connect to complete the ARC in the example with your coworker Taylor.

- "OK, just so I'm clear, you're feeling like the new kid and haven't been fully welcomed to the team. Makes sense. Thanks for sharing that. I'll work on that."
- "So I understand you correctly, the disconnection from the rest of the team causes misunderstandings. OK, I'll work on building in more remote teambuilding. Thank you!"

Deep Dive:

PSYCHOLOGICAL SAFETY TIPS

Here are some other tips to create psychological safety at work:

- Set a no-phones-in-meetings policy.
- Demonstrate that showing compassion for others is appreciated.
- As your team is arriving at a decision, deliberately ask for questions, different viewpoints, and considerations that have not yet been voiced.
- Thank people for their contributions during brainstorming sessions, even if their ideas aren't used.
- Create trust by modeling consistency, accuracy, and kindness.
- Own up to the mistakes you've made and celebrate failures as learnings.
- Regularly ask employees what they've done that didn't work out as expected and what they learned from those experiences.
- Have a zero-tolerance policy for negativity, which can become contagious and spread to others.
- Consult all of the team when decision-making. Ask for their input, thoughts, and feedback. Make sure that everyone's voice has been heard.

Roll out unconscious/implicit bias training for everyone

Most of this book focuses on changing systems within organizations so they are more just and equitable, so those systems include and reflect the beautiful diversity of our world. System and policy change will ultimately move the needle most quickly towards your critical DEI initiatives.

But systems are ultimately run by people. And for DEI initiatives to truly stick, people need to change, too. This behavior change generally starts with some form of education, often unconscious bias training. You may remember that I introduced the concept of unconscious bias back in Chapter 1.

Unconscious bias training is a foundational part of any DEI initiative, but over the past few years, it's gotten a bad rap. There are headlines that declare, "The unconscious bias training you've been told to do won't work" and warns against "The dangers of unconscious bias training."

A key message of unconscious bias training is that we all do it. We all have bias. And yes, while that's true, very few people want to be told they have bias. *Even when they're told that everybody has bias.*

That's why those headlines declare that unconscious bias training doesn't work. Unconscious bias training often shuts people down right away.

My approach to unconscious bias training is a little different, and dare I say—more effective. Instead of saying, "We all have bias," I'd rather say, "We all make assumptions." It goes down a little easier. We share small assumptions that we've made about others, and then share small assumptions others have made about us. And yes, in my presentations, I talk about the time my gaydar was off. Way off. Whoops.

These are mostly harmless stories, often embarrassing. There is laughter in the stories and we loosen up. We open up.

Then the stories get a little bit bigger, a bit more uncomfortable. The time someone assumed that I'm the "man" in my lesbian relationship is also brought up. That time the Starbucks manager assumed two Black men waiting in the store were up to no good, then called the cops.

Suddenly, people within the room (or the virtual room) start sharing. There's empathy in the room. There are some somber nods. Everyone is listening.

Then the stories turn to workplace assumptions, and we dig in deeper on the causes and effects of these assumptions. And we address solutions!

This reframing of unconscious bias as just another type of assumption is powerful and relatable. In my consulting firm, we present this in two and a half hour workshops with variations for leaders and individual contributors.

When we strip away the negativity of the term unconscious bias, people open up. They start to see all the assumptions we make about others every day. Many of those assumptions are incredibly helpful and timesaving. But some of them put others in a box and hold them back. Using the term "unconscious bias" shuts the door for many people before they even see what's in the room. And we want them to see what's in the room!

Most of the time assumptions are accidental, little habits our personal experiences have ingrained into our minds and our way of being. The truth of the matter is, we all make assumptions. We all have bias. But that doesn't make it OK. We still need to do the work to change these biases, and when we reframe the conversation, we get more traction toward real change. And I think we can all admit we want real change.

The other problem with many unconscious bias trainings is that they lack the critical, "Now what?" Many of these workshops lack real solutions besides providing simple awareness. Simple awareness is indeed critical, but it must go hand in hand with systemic changes.

Many of the "solutions" to unconscious bias that I speak about during a workshop are themes explored throughout this book. Again, when we change the system or the policy to be inclusive, we reduce the likelihood of human bias.

Unconscious bias training is critical, but it should not be the end-all and be-all. Start with unconscious bias training and keep going!

Train customer-facing employees

John Timmerman, former VP of Operations for Ritz-Carlton, once said, *"At the end of the day, our bottom line is in the hands of our front line."* He's right; the front line is where the rubber meets the road. [161]

All industries can learn from this, and while the standards and requirements for anti-harassment training vary state by state, a proactive approach helps an organization become defensible from future liability.

One challenge organizations face is that they seldom bring unconscious bias training down to the front line, exposing the brand to a host of possible bias-related incidents.

We define the front line fairly broadly—anyone in the business of sales or customer service. The front line obviously includes those in retail and hospitality, but also includes those in professional services, and those who work in business development. If you have employees who sell or service customers, clients, guests, patients, students, and more—then you have a front line.

We realize that frontline teams are harder to reach for training. And it's true: they may be on the floor or at a front desk without easy access to an unconscious bias eLearning tool. They may be in the field visiting clients, or they may work remotely, where eLearning is the only option. Front line employees often move quickly, sometimes only interacting with a customer or client for moments at a time—just long enough for a mistaken assumption or a microaggression.

Frontline employees are also asked to respond to bias incidents—customer on customer bias—yet often don't receive training in how to respond, short of calling the police.

Unconscious bias training for frontline employees must take all of these factors into consideration: It must be actionable and teachable by managers. It should be scalable. It should speak to all learning methods. It should get to the point, but do so without merely "checking the box." And it should do so quickly.

I'm a bit obsessed with what happens at the front line, because I think about the ripple effect....

Take for example, a customer or a client experiences a negative assumption from a frontline employee. It's accidental, of course, but it's painful, and a reminder of how they are different from the dominant culture. Microaggressions are often described as "death by a thousand paper cuts"—they are little but painful, and they add up—and people get fed up.

The employee's recovery is awkward and ineffective.
The customer/client may react badly towards your employee or others.
You may lose customers or clients.
You may be the subject of a viral incident.
The customer/client may treat others badly in their lives, because it's how they've been treated.

Sometimes the roles are reversed and the negative assumption is made by your customer against your employee. That's terrible as well, and frontline employees should be trained on appropriate responses, how to handle different situations, and how to be aware of their own biases.

Train employees on LGBTQ+ inclusion

LGBTQ+ Parents

Right now in the United States, 20% of same-sex couples are raising children under the age of 18. Surveys tell us that about 50% of gay men and lesbians expect to have children in the future. With marriage equality the law of the land, having a family seems like the next logical step for many LGBTQ+ couples. This can have a profound impact on your customer service. [162]

Although families have been increasingly diverse (many with single parents or children being raised by grandparents), many businesses fail to include LGBTQ+ families in their customer service training. Here are a few tips to ensure that LGBTQ+ families are included.

Train your employees to interact with all guests, including children, neutrally, in order to avoid any assumptions about the child's parents. This means that if the child is interacting with one of your employees, the employee should under no circumstances make a reference to the mother or father, but rather to the parent. If the employee references mommy, and the child doesn't have a mommy, that comment will make the child feel isolated and stigmatized.

Your employee should not have to be corrected by a child. This can, of course, lead to a loss of business. As with gender, the best approach is neutral words. For example, an employee asking a single child, "Do you need help finding your mommy?" could be stigmatizing for a child with two dads. A better approach is, "Do you need help finding your parent?" [163]

Deep Dive:

LGBTQ+ INCLUSIVE FORMS

Change your internal forms to make it easier for your front line to be LGBTQ+ inclusive:

- Consider whether you actually need to collect someone's sex on forms, and how relevant that information actually is.
- If it is, update your internal policies to allow for a box beyond male or female on forms. Include "other" and/or "X."
- Update your internal policies to allow for titles beyond Mr., Mrs., Miss, Ms., Dr. and include Mx. (the gender-neutral honorific).
- If you run a medical office, gym, school, camp, museum, or otherwise have a form that parents/families must fill out, remember that the form should not say mother's name and father's name, but rather inclusive language such as "Name(s) of Parents/Guardians."

Transgender-Inclusive Customer Service

Many systemic barriers (like a lack of protection from discrimination) make it difficult for transgender people to feel safe walking through the world—both as employees and as customers. To be *Inclusive 360*, your organization must train all employees on transgender inclusion to create safe spaces for both customers and other employees. Training your customer-facing team is critical to creating those safe spaces.

For transgender people, being asked to show a driver's license or other identity card can be incredibly stressful. Each state has its own policy regarding changing names and gender markers. For example, where I live, in Illinois, someone can change their gender marker simply by signing a form attesting to their gender identity, with no medical signature or documentation required. In Alabama, in order to change their gender marker, they must provide a letter from a surgeon or an updated birth certificate saying that they've had gender confirmation surgery.

This is much more difficult to do, especially for the transgender people that choose to not have surgery or can't have surgery because of financial or medical barriers. Changing one's name on an ID is also a complex process, typically involving legal notices in newspapers and court appearances as well as large costs, depending on the state.

California wanted to ensure that all registered voters have a seamless voting experience in 2020, so they trained poll workers on best practices to be inclusive of transgender and non-binary voters. Poll workers received training on situations such as if someone's appearance seems different from the name on the registration list.

The biggest part of the poll worker training is how to respond to voters whose gender identity, expression, or pronouns don't match their name on the voter rolls. There was also an information campaign to ensure that transgender and non-binary voters know their rights.

"Elections officials have a duty to facilitate the participation of all eligible voters," said former California Secretary of State Alex Padilla in a statement. *"California is proud to be proactive in protecting the voting rights of LGBTQ+ voters and fostering an inclusive democracy."*[164]

The NYC Taxi and Limousine Commission sent its 100,000 drivers "inclusive language tips" to be more supportive of transgender and non-binary passengers. This is an incredible best practice for frontline employees like drivers.

The "Inclusive Language Tips" document was emailed to more than 100,000 licensed drivers, according to CNN, and includes advice such as asking passengers what their pronouns are, not assuming pronouns based on appearance or name, and apologizing if a mistake is made. The email originated from the commission's Office of Inclusion, formed in 2018 to combat service refusals by taxis and other for-hire vehicles.

The Inclusive Language Tips document calls out potential offenses, like referring to someone as "it" or "he-she," and encourages drivers to "use gender-neutral pronouns such as they or ze" if they are unsure of the individual's gender identity. [165]

Phone Customer Service

When one of your employees is speaking to a customer on the phone and pulling up their account information, they may find that the account information references a male name when the voice on the phone sounds very female. Or vice versa. Or the person on the phone doesn't identify as male or female yet your data puts them in one of those boxes. This unfortunately leads to lots of awkward phone conversations and requests to be transferred to a manager.

A transgender woman had taken the time to update her Santander bank account with the correct title, correct name, and correct gender, and ensured the bank's paperwork all reflected her gender identity. Yet, when she went to access her account on the phone, an employee said that she sounds like a man and froze her out.

The employee assumed that this woman was a man just based on that person's voice. I'm sure the employee was well-meaning but assumed the woman's gender. And of course, that assumption made the news. For all customer-facing employees, transgender-inclusive training is a good idea. It's a hard habit to break, but we simply cannot assume a person's gender based on appearance or voice. [166]

A few years ago, my firm conducted a customer experience survey of transgender and gender-nonconforming people. Here are some comments from our survey respondents:

> *"The phone is always the most challenging. I understand but please listen to me when I ask for you to correct it. When I explained I was not a sir he asked if I would rather be called brother."*

"I get, 'I can't give you any information on this account. The account holder is female and you are obviously male.' I get referred to managers a lot."

"I'm often refused entry to things or access to my accounts because my voice doesn't match my feminine first name. I've even been TOLD by customer service that I'm NOT who I say I am."

Phone customer service creates challenges with transgender people but does not need to create major challenges for your institution.

Deep Dive:

LGBTQ+ INCLUSIVE CUSTOMER SERVICE TRAINING

Training your customer-facing employees to sensitively interact with the LGBTQ+ community is another area your institution can show inclusiveness. Here are some best practices:

- Avoid use of "sir" and "ma'am." Greetings can be very friendly by just saying, "How can I help you?"
- Similarly, if they have a feminine gender expression yet a male gender marker on their ID, ask other qualifying questions such as date or place of birth to verify identity.
- Mistakes happen. If your associate slips up and uses the wrong pronoun or uses "sir" or "ma'am" inappropriately, apologize quickly with a comment like: "I'm sorry for using the wrong pronoun/name. I did not mean to disrespect you." Then move on without over-apologizing and turning the interaction into a big hullaballoo!
- Don't feel the need to transfer the customer to a manager unless there are other issues that arise—it makes the transgender customer feel marginalized.

Offer other workshops

Educating employees on differences across identities is essential to deliver on the promises made by diversity. Business Resource Groups can be a great driver for this education, although, in most cases, we recommend bringing in outside facilitators to offer a third party perspective.

Our firm regularly delivers workshops, and our contacts at organizations are often BRG leaders. These are some of the workshops we believe are valuable to help employees better understand each other to leverage the power of their differences:

- **Antiracism 101 workshop:** this workshop defines key terms, illustrates historic and modern examples of systemic racism, and provides ways individuals and organizations can be active antiracists.
- **LGBTQ+ 101 workshop:** this addresses key terms, important public policies, and best practices in allyship.
- **Transgender 101 workshop:** this digs deeper and explores the transgender and non-binary communities in more detail, providing best practices in allyship. This workshop is typically led by a transgender presenter.
- **Cultural Competency workshop:** this workshop addresses cultural norms in different parts of the world and provides key tips for understanding appropriate body language and cultural cues.

To ensure that learning sticks with employees, ask your workshop facilitator to provide a tip sheet with key takeaways and a discussion guide for managers to facilitate continued employee learning.

Behavior change is hard and should not be treated as a box to be checked. Continuing education is key. A continual combination of the offerings throughout this chapter will set your organization up for success.

Inclusive 360 Action Steps

☐ Require all managers and leaders attend inclusive leadership workshops.

☐ Require all employees attend a certain number of workshops on allyship annually, and offer workshops regularly.

☐ Deploy LGBTQ+ inclusive customer service training for all customer facing and call center employees.

Keep learning:

- Book: Overcoming Bias by Tiffany Jana and Matthew Freeman
- Book: How to Be an Inclusive Leader by Jennifer Brown
- Book: Unleashed by Frances Frei and Anne Morriss
- Book: The 5 Disciplines of Inclusive Leadership by Andrés Tapia and Alina Polonskaia

THE COMBINATION OF data and storytelling can change behavior because it appeals to both the heart and the mind. To successfully get buy-in at every stage of your DEI journey, you must thoughtfully present both arguments.

CHAPTER 12

Express Yourself
Inclusive Employee Benefits and Expression

Establish your baseline

YOUR EMPLOYEES WILL work their tails off for your organization if you take great care of them and give them the space to authentically express their identities. It sounds basic, but inclusive benefits and personal expression policies are simply a form of positive reinforcement, as old as Pavlov's 1903 study of dogs.

Of course, inclusive benefits and expression policies are a bit more complex than dog treats, especially when working to create an inclusive and psychologically safe environment.

Research shows that employees who are given greater freedom of self-expression (including showing visible tattoos, fully expressing their personality, etc.) have higher retention and customer satisfaction rates.

Michael French from the University of Miami surveyed more than 2,000 people throughout the U.S. and found those with tattoos were no less hirable for customer-facing jobs than those without. Employers are slowly becoming more accepting of tattoos as tattoos become more common. In a tight job market, employers understand that policies against tattoos may turn away quality employees. The U.S. Marines now allows recruits with visible tattoos as long as they're not visible on their face or neck.[168]

Take a careful look at your own organization's human resources policies and benefits by following the ARC.

ASK.

For each policy and benefit, Ask:

- Is there anyone who is not being served?
- Do employees at every level of the organization receive these benefits?
- Do our policies exclude anyone?

RESPECT.

Respect the answers. Respect the data. Stay true. If you have benefits that exclude transgender people, part-time workers, parents or single people, your benefits are not inclusive. If your policies for dress code exclude anyone, they're not inclusive.

CONNECT.

Connect the answers to specific solutions that will make policies and benefits more inclusive. Solutions like:

Commit to floating holidays

In addition to traditional paid organizational holidays like Labor Day and Memorial Day, I'd suggest that you also offer floating holidays.

Floating holidays are days employees can use at their discretion to celebrate a "non-mainstream" holiday. For example, 22 million Americans celebrate Hannukah, 12.5 million Americans celebrate Kwanzaa, and 3.5 million celebrate Eid-Al-Fidr, but these days are seldom included in most Paid Time Off (PTO).[169]

Floating holidays can also be used for holidays that are not recognized in all states, like Juneteenth. Juneteenth is a holiday that commemorates June 19, the day the news of U.S. slave emancipation reached Texas (the last state to get the news) at the end of the Civil War.[170] In 2021, Juneteenth was added as a federal holiday, even though states may choose not to observe it.

In 2020, many organizations, including Nike and Twitter, went beyond including Juneteenth as a floating holiday and actually made it an official paid company holiday. This shows Black employees that they matter and is an opportunity to educate other employees on Black history.

Get inclusive with parental leave

In the United States, many Americans who welcome a child don't receive paid time off. The U.S. is one of just eight countries that doesn't have a law mandating some paid parental leave.[171]

The state of Oregon, in a bi-partisan effort, passed the most comprehensive family leave policy in the country. The law allows all workers, including low-wage workers, to earn 100% of their income for 12 weeks while caring for a new child, a sick family member, or after suffering domestic violence.[172]

Fortunately, many organizations are filling in the leave gap by offering robust benefits for new parents. The best practice in parental leave is to offer all parents equal benefits. More and more families have both parents (if there are two) actively involved in newborn care.

The old standard for organizations was 12 weeks of maternal leave, with some organizations offering no benefits for fathers or non-biological mothers. The average for technology organizations is now 18 weeks, but Spotify and Etsy offer 26 weeks of paid leave to new moms and dads. [173]

The gold standard in the United States, however, is Netflix. The company offers new parents 52 weeks of paid leave after the arrival of a child—including after adoption.[174]

Hourly employees who work in shifts often receive no parental leave benefits. The restaurant Sweetgreen set the standard for how hourly shift workers are treated. Sweetgreen offers five months of paid parental leave for all employees, including hourly shift workers in restaurants.[175]

Starbucks provides its baristas with six weeks of paid parental leave, and Target offers all 350,000 of its employees medical leave coverages, including retail workers who are hourly and part time. Those folks may now access up to four weeks of paid leave to care for a newborn or sick family member. They can also receive 20 days of included child care or elder care.[176]

Support working parents

While many organizations provided their employees' children free access to virtual summer camps, virtual afterschool programs, and virtual family events during the COVID-19 pandemic, the best-in-class organizations also upped their childcare benefits and made them permanent.

To support working parents who have kids in remote learning during the COVID-19 pandemic, Bank of America introduced a daily childcare reimbursement of $75 or $100, depending on the employee's salary, for children up to 12-years-old and children with special needs through 21-years-old through December 31, 2020.[177]

Many parents are familiar with the stress of having a child care provider cancel at the last minute. Through partnerships with childcare centers like Bright Horizons, more companies such as Starbucks, Bank of America, Accenture and more offer backup childcare for employees. For example, Accenture provides 120 hours of subsidized backup care for a newborn's first year and 80 hours every year thereafter.[178]

KPMG quadrupled the number of days employees can use the firm's backup care program, greatly expanded its network of discounted childcare centers, and greatly expanded its network of discounted tutoring, academic support, test prep, and homework assistance programs.[179]

Target expanded its backup family-care program to all employees and waived eligibility requirements. In 2019, they opened this program (with 20 days of benefits) to all employees, including frontline employees. In 2020, they made the announcement that copays for childcare and other requirements were waived for all employees.[180]

Hilton, Unilever, and IBM are some of the companies that have a partnership with Milk Stork. Through this program, nursing parents who are traveling for work can, at no charge, ship or carry (on flights) their breast milk, solving an important problem for many traveling parents with newborns.[181]

And finally, consider doing what Facebook does: new parents receive $4,000 in cash to help defray any new baby costs. Employees can use this money at their discretion, even for take-out food.

Provide transgender-inclusive medical care

If your organization wants to be best-in-class and an attractive place to work for underrepresented employees, a critical employee benefit is transgender-inclusive health care coverage. An astounding 71% of Fortune 500 companies now have some level of health care coverage.

This figure comes from the Human Rights Campaign (HRC), which releases an annual Corporate Equality Index (CEI)—a barometer of a company's LGBTQ+ inclusivity. To achieve a 100% score on the CEI, companies must offer their employees transgender-inclusive health coverage. According to HRC, great transgender-inclusive health care benefits include the following: [182]

- Short term medical leave
- Mental health benefits
- Pharmaceutical coverage (e.g., for hormone replacement therapies)
- Coverage for medical visits or laboratory services
- Coverage for transition-related surgeries
- Insurance coverage of routine, chronic, or urgent non-transition (for example, prostate exams for transgender women and pelvic/gynecological exams for transgender men must be covered)

The dollar maximums on transgender coverage must meet or exceed $75,000; however, the best practice is for no annual or lifetime dollar cap. In addition to providing this medical coverage, I suggest that you identify a specific point of contact at the insurer who is equipped to handle all transgender coverage questions. You'll then be ready if an employee comes out to you as transgender and wants to medically transition.

Offer mental health support

Organizations are increasingly aware of the importance of employee well-being and mental health. Some organizations, such as Tyson Foods, were keenly in tune to this even before the COVID-19 pandemic.

The company has a 100 employee Chaplain Program with multi-denominational chaplains who support employees through transition, stress, and even celebratory life events. A chaplain may help employees address personal matters such as housing and child care needs, or may just be a safe and confidential sounding board. This program helps employees stay more present and engaged at work.[183]

"People tell us all sorts of things about their life," Karen Diefendorf, Director of Chaplain Services said. *"It might begin with I've just put mom or dad in a nursing home or maybe somebody in their family is going on hospice.... Life comes with us in the door. So all those myriad of things that you think about, it happens in our plants. And so our chaplains are there to be a resource to help people process life."*[184]

Intel's Warm-Line is a Winner

A few years ago, Intel realized that it was having difficulty retaining women and BIPOC. In response, they created the WarmLine, a confidential resource line where trained professionals can help employees address their workplace struggles. The WarmLine has worked so well that 82% of those who call have stayed with the company, particularly among Black, Hispanic, and Native American employees.

The WarmLine hotline is operated by case managers on Intel's Global Diversity and Inclusion team. The goal is to resolve any issues that arise, whether that's mediating a sit down with a manager or supporting an employee looking for more career growth. Because of the Warm-Line, employees have received career development advice, changed departments, and received pay adjustments.

The WarmLine has responded to over 20,000 cases, which provide valuable data to the company, including which manager or department has the highest percentage of cases and issues women and minorities face.

"We have used the WarmLine data to not only create training and educational programs but also used it to develop playbooks tailored to every business unit so leaders can understand their organization's top challenges," said Barbara Whye, Intel's former chief diversity and inclusion officer.[185]

Other organizations took a more traditional approach to mental health benefits until the COVID-19 pandemic. The combination of the pandemic and racial trauma made 2020 particularly taxing on Black and Asian people.

With more employees reporting feelings of isolation, disengagement, trauma, and stress, many organizations, like Condé Nast, began offering memberships or sessions on TalkSpace, an app-based platform where users can have telehealth conversations with licensed therapists.[186]

The organizations that realize the importance of supporting employee mental health will be the ones that are able to successfully retain underrepresented employees and leverage the power of diversity.[187]

Provide educational benefits

Educational benefits can help organizations grow their skilled work forces. Walmart has one program to help its high school-aged employees finish school, and get college-ready, and another program to pay for college for all other employees.

Walmart's goal is to attract more high school students as employees and train the next generation of leaders. They provide free ACT and SAT preparation and up to seven hours of free college credit. Once employees have graduated high school, they can move into their Live Better U college program. This free college program is for all employees (even part time and supply chain) who have worked there at least 90 days. Part of that program provides access to Guild Education, an education benefits platform, that provides academic counselors to help Walmart associates with everything from the application process to choosing the right degree.

Students can get degrees online from universities such as Purdue and the University of New Hampshire. The program covers degrees in the fields of technology, business or supply chain management, cybersecurity, computer science, computer and network security, and computing technology. Currently 7,500 Walmart employees are enrolled.

Walmart also covers the full cost of fees, and books. With this program, Walmart wants to ensure that its associates can earn a debt-free college degree.[188]

Chipotle also covers 100% of tuition costs up front for 75 types of business and technology degrees via Guild Education. This program builds on another of Chipotle's educational programs, which allows workers to be reimbursed up to $5,250 a year for tuition at any school.

To qualify, Chipotle employees must have worked at the company for at least three months and work at least 15 hours per week. Chipotle reports 90% higher retention among Chipotle employees who participate in the education benefits program.[189]

Tuition benefits like these help companies build up a workforce that can then take on other jobs at the company that might require more advanced skills, like technical and engineering jobs. Tuition benefits develop a pipeline of loyal employees that also expands the set of candidates that you can hire for those more technical positions.

Offer a four-day workweek

Microsoft tested a four-day workweek in Japan for the entire month of August 2019 and saw productivity increase by 40% from July. This is measured by sales per employee.

More than 90% of Microsoft's 2,280 employees in Japan reported they were impacted by the new measures. In addition to this, the company was also able to save on other resources, such as electricity, by shutting down earlier each week. [190]

Pre-pandemic, Shake Shack moved its managers to a four-day workweek consisting of four, ten-hour days. The company tested a pilot in 2019 that has since been expanded to a third of Shake Shack locations. One of the unexpected benefits is more women applying to be managers. Shake Shack's president, Tara Comonte, says staff love the benefit, *"Being able to take their kids to school a day a week, or one day less of having to pay for day care, for example. It was a way to increase flexibility. Corporate environments have had flexible work policies for a while now. That's not so easy to do in the restaurant business."*

Natalie Nagele, CEO of software company Wildbit, has also found success with a four day workweek. *"We had shipped more features than we had in recent years, we felt more productive, the quality of our work increased. So then we just kept going with it,"* Nagele says. Personally, she says, it gives her time to rest her brain, which helps solve complex problems: *"You can ask my team, there's multiple times where somebody is like, 'On Sunday morning, I woke up and... I figured it out.' "*[191]

Support your veterans

Bank of America provides robust benefits to support veterans and their families. Bank of America also provides tools and resources that address common challenges veterans face when transitioning from military service to civilian life. These best-in-class benefits include support for mental health initiatives, financial education, and leadership development.

Bank of America's Business Resource Group, Military Support & Assistance Group (MSAG), provides networking, mentoring, volunteer events, and information forums. As a result of these programs, more than 500 veterans and military spouses hold leadership positions at the company. MSAG also includes a military spouse group which provides resources and support for veteran spouses who work at the bank.[192]

Establish transgender-inclusive policies

When you give your employees and customers the opportunity to self-identify their gender and pronouns, everyone wins. Your employees can refer to information on gender and pronouns rather than making assumptions about their co-workers or customers. Employees may feel more able to be authentic at work.

Policies that allow customers and employees to self-identify are an important best practice. Not only does it send a signal to your customers that your organization is paying attention to the diversity of its community, but it also represents a powerful step towards inclusion, especially given that 31% of Gen Z Americans identify as LGBTQ+.[193]

- Allow customer-facing employees to share their pronouns on their name badges.
- Add pronouns to email signatures, right below the name.
- Add pronouns to LinkedIn profiles.
- During meetings where everyone doesn't know each other, include pronouns in introductions, and personal names used in videoconferencing.
- Invite folks to add their pronouns on name badges at in-person events.

T-Mobile allows its retail employees to include pronouns on their name badges or have the phrase "ask me my pronouns." This proactive move will reduce the risk of transgender and non-binary employees being misgendered by guests.

This move came about when an employee who was transitioning told their manager that they didn't want to be referred to as he or she. The employee was afraid of being misgendered by guests or other employees. The manager then reached out to T-Mobile's corporate office to suggest a simple solution.

"This is just another way for employees to express who they are, in addition to already having the option to add their military affiliation and up to four languages that they speak," T-Mobile said in a blog post.[194]

Starbucks and Target both offer employees the option to use pronoun pins as well.

Offer flexible expression and dress code

Sometimes inclusion can be as simple as having fewer rules about employee behavior and expression.

Many companies are realizing that personal office décor is an important form of self-expression. More progressive companies encourage employees to decorate with pictures, posters, murals, trophies and anything else they want—and trusts their employees to decide what is and is not appropriate. Decorations can become conversation starters, which in turn can strengthen relationships. This freedom of expression allows clients and co-workers to find common ground and build more authentic relationships.

Although gendered dress is the default formal dress code in many organizations, some places in the U.S., like California and New York City, prohibit gender-specific dress codes. For maximum employee inclusion, less is more in your own dress code.

Up until 2015, General Motors had a 10-page, strict dress code policy. CEO Mary Barra updated it to two simple words: "dress appropriately."[195]

In a win for gender expression, Virgin Atlantic Airways told female flight attendants they no longer have to wear makeup, and now have a choice between pants and skirts. Female flight attendants can wear whichever they prefer. Airlines have traditionally been particularly stringent on employee dress codes, often enforcing codes that were created without consideration to gender diversity and gender expression. To be inclusive of gender diversity, this is an excellent best practice for any industry with uniformed employees.[196]

Even the Mayor of Mexico City has jumped on board. Mayor Claudia Sheinbaum changed a public school policy requiring boys uniforms and girls uniforms. Now all students can choose the uniform that best fits their gender expression. *"Boys can wear skirts if they want and girls can wear trousers if they want,"* Mayor Sheinbaum said. She added that the measure would create, *"...a condition of equality, of equity."* [197]

Inclusive dress codes should also permit braids, dreadlocks, Afros, and other hairstyles popular with Black folks. These styles are banned by many organizations. UPS only overturned its ban in 2020. As of publication, 11 states have passed the CROWN (Create a Respectful and Open World for Natural Hair) Act to ban hair discrimination.

The combination of these benefits will have a powerful impact on your employee experience, increase retention, and set up your organization to be deemed a desirable place to work for underrepresented talent.

Inclusive 360 Action Steps

☐ As you move into solutions-mode, consider which ideas can be quick wins? Which ideas will have a direct impact on the organization's business objectives? Which ideas require external support?

☐ Choose at least 10 of the best-in-class benefits I wrote about and change your policies accordingly.

Keep learning:

- Book: Transgender in the Workplace by Vanessa Sheridan
- Book: Building an Inclusive Organization by Stephen Frost and Raafi-Karim Alidina

RESEARCH SHOWS THAT employees who are given greater freedom of self-expression (including showing visible tattoos, fully expressing their personality, etc.) have higher retention and customer satisfaction rates. Sometimes inclusion can be as simple as having fewer rules about employee behavior and expression.

CHAPTER 13:

9 to 5
Random Acts
of Inclusion

Inclusive facilities

IN MY RESEARCH for this book, I found so many inspiring examples of inclusion that don't necessarily fit neatly elsewhere. Let's start with the easy stuff that you can prioritize implementing this week.

Transgender people should be allowed to use the restroom of their gender identity. Period. This should not be debatable.

Yet, unfortunately, it is.

In the U.S., so-called "bathroom bills" have been introduced to explicitly require everyone to use the restroom of the gender listed on their birth certificate. For someone who is cisgender, this is no big deal. For someone who is transgender or non-binary and does not have a new birth certificate that reflects their actual gender identity, this is ridiculous! Imagine birth certificate checks at restroom doors!

And just imagine a big, burly, transgender man in a woman's restroom. That's what could happen if transgender people followed these laws. Due to public outcry and corporate protests (such as the NBA deciding to move its 2017 All-Star Game from Charlotte, North Carolina), many of the anti-transgender restroom laws, like one in North Carolina, have been repealed.

Still, at the time of publication, transgender people (and gays and lesbians—or those suspected to be) can be denied access to restrooms (and any other public accommodation) in parts of 28 states. And in 2021 alone, more than 16 anti-LGBTQ+ laws have been passed in various U.S. states.

Why does this matter to your organization?

Organizations can build employee and customer loyalty (and just do the right thing) by providing transgender-inclusive restroom policies and facilities.

This starts with a policy that specifically states that everyone (both customers and employees) is allowed to use the restroom of their actual gender identity. Here's a sample of an employee policy:

"All employees have a right to safe and appropriate restroom facilities. Employees will have access to the restroom corresponding to their actual gender identity, regardless of the employee's sex assigned at birth. That is, transgender women must be permitted to use the women's restroom, and transgender men must be permitted to use the men's restroom. That decision should be left to the transgender employee to determine the most appropriate and safest option for them.

Some employees—transgender or cisgender—may desire additional privacy. Where possible, an employer will make available an all-gender single-stall restroom that can be used by any employee who has a need for increased privacy, regardless of the underlying reason. For example, if any employee does not want to share a multi-person restroom with a transgender coworker, they can make use of this kind of option, if available.

And a customer policy:

All individuals have a right to use restroom facilities that correspond to the individual's gender identity, regardless of the individual's sex assigned at birth. Our organization has a policy of non-discrimination on the basis of sex, sexual orientation, gender identity, or gender expression/presentation."

Or this simple line from Target:

"We welcome transgender team members and guests to use the restroom or fitting room facility that corresponds with their gender identity."

Target faced a boycott by conservatives over this policy. Their response was to spend $20 million to ensure each U.S. store has at least one all-gender single-stall restroom. That's allyship in action.[198]

All-gender restrooms are not just best practices for big businesses; they are recommended for all businesses. In fact, 170,000+ businesses have communicated to the world that they have all-gender restrooms. Yelp allows businesses to indicate they have all-gender restrooms via their business dashboard on Yelp.com. Anyone can search Yelp to find the businesses in their area with all-gender restrooms. Transgender people feel more comfortable using a public restroom while also making sure they aren't harassed by random people for simply using the restroom. While this is great, it sure would be nice for them not to have to check Yelp!

Transgender and non-binary people are keenly aware of where they can use the restroom in public. There are even websites that track all-gender restrooms around the United States. Transgender people want to feel safe. And they know they can always go to Target. That brand loyalty is priceless.

Some states and cities like New York City, Philadelphia, and all of California now have laws which require that public single-stall restrooms be designated as all-gender or gender neutral (instead of men's rooms and women's rooms). This includes restrooms in government buildings, restaurants, and more.

This law may be designed to be transgender-inclusive, but I am thrilled because I've waited too many times for the single-stall women's room to open up while the men's room was vacant!

If your premises has any single-stall restrooms, don't just wait for the state to change its laws! Be proactive and rebrand all of your single-stall restrooms to be all-gender.

If you want to take it a step further, consider rebranding ALL of your restrooms to be all-gender. This includes multi-stall restrooms. Condé Nast rebranded all of their multi-stall restrooms as all-gender and still indicate which restrooms have urinals.

ALL GENDER
RESTROOM

Anyone can use this restroom,
regardless of gender identity
or expression

Beyond that, Condé Nast and other companies now provide pads and tampons in all restrooms (yes, even the ones with urinals)—because it's not just women who get periods. This is the optimal best practice for all-gender restrooms.[199]

While you're rebranding and updating your restrooms, don't forget about the changing tables—remember, dads change diapers, too.

In 2015, Ashton Kutcher went to Facebook to complain about the lack of diaper changing tables in public men's rooms. He wrote that he had yet to encounter a changing table in the public bathrooms he visits. He offered to give a social media shout-out to the first business where he found a diapering table in the men's room.

In an interview on his website, Kutcher said, *"I would like my daughter to experience a world where gender doesn't dictate one's responsibility or limit one's opportunity,"* he said, adding, *"Having changing tables in men's rooms is just a tiny step in the process of rectifying legacy gender dis-*

crimination. Men who are aware of this bias want to participate equally in the child care process and our society should support that. It's time to get our hands dirty." [200]

If your organization has any public facilities, please have an all-gender single-stall restroom with a changing table. And if you don't have an all-gender single-stall restroom, then the best practice is to include a changing table in both men's and women's rooms.

Make your meetings inclusive

Nothing gets done in the workplace without meetings, yet meetings are often cringe-worthy for one reason or another. And meetings are spaces ripe for exclusionary experiences. They're not deliberately exclusive, but often are spaces where underrepresented people report not feeling heard or recognized.

When each employee in a meeting shares at least once and the team is empathetic, the team performs better. When leaders and facilitators actively promote turn-taking, model empathy, and are deliberately inclusive of introverts, the whole team shines.

In Google's groundbreaking study on their highest-performing teams, other traits they found in those teams include equality in distribution of conversational turn-taking and high average social sensitivity. [201]

How does this play out in real life? Here are some best practices for all meetings:

> **Consider the attendee list.** Before setting your meeting, think about the attendee list. Is it the same people as always? Is there value to inviting new voices or other diverse perspectives to expand the ideas being shared?

Write and send a detailed agenda to all participants at least 24 hours in advance. Consider whether the agenda has any specific diversity, equity, and inclusion commitments.

List agenda items as questions, not simply topics, and encourage everyone to review prior to the meeting. This gives introverts a chance to process information in advance, outside of the pressure of a loud social setting. Enlist leaders and allies to model inclusion and hold them accountable for making space for their female, remote, underrepresented, and/or introverted counterparts to contribute, and contribute early on, to the conversation.

Make everyone feel welcome by briefly inviting each attendee to introduce themselves and share their pronouns when there are new attendees. After doing so, I encourage you to share briefly why each has been included in this meeting. This helps everyone feel valued and included.

Lay some ground rules such as a "no cell phones" rule (except on breaks) and a "no talking over each other" rule. Give attendees permission to speak up and call out interruptions. You can lead by example if you witness an interruption by using phrases like, "Wait a sec, I want to hear the rest of Jackie's point before we add to it." Assume people who interrupt someone mean no malice—they don't do it to be intentionally exclusive. Repeat interrupters should be taken aside separately to point out the behavior.

Prompt input from everyone with questions such as "What are your thoughts?" or "How would you approach this problem?"

Praise often. When someone shares a great idea, quickly acknowledge it publicly. There's a tendency for unacknowledged great ideas to be given credit to another, louder voice.

Rotate notetaking so no one person is stuck in the "adminis-trative" role. This often happens to women and subconscious-ly perpetuates the stereotype that women aren't leaders. If you have one employee who tends to talk a lot or dominate conversation, ask that person to be the scribe. This role gives them more responsibility to listen and creates a space for oth-ers to share.

For more difficult discussion topics, **require a few minutes of silence** to process the question quietly before inviting at-tendees to share their ideas. This gives introverts more space to formulate their thoughts before sharing them amidst the louder voices in the room.

Thank everyone for their contributions.

Deep Dive:

INCLUSIVE REMOTE MEETINGS

In my firm's own work, we've found remote meetings to be surpris-ingly effective, especially when facilitated with an inclusive lens. Here are some best practices we've found in our many virtual trainings and other meetings:

- Be mindful of rotating time zones so certain people aren't al-ways stuck with early morning or evening meetings.
- Encourage cameras on, but don't require it. You don't want those with inadequate home office setups to feel embarrassed.
- Encourage people to share pronouns. In most platforms, you can pre-set your last name with pronouns. Zoom allows you to add your pronouns to your user profile.
- Start with an icebreaker or non-work group activity or discussion.

- Assign one person to monitor the chat for questions and key insights. Rotate that role each meeting.
- Invite participants to use the chat actively to share questions and insights.
- To set introverts up for success, use breakout rooms to enable pairs and small group interactions.
- When you ask the group a challenging question to discuss, give them 60 seconds of silence, and then ask them to type quickly in chat. This "chat storm" approach can yield powerful results and work well for introverts, too.
- Consider installing a closed-captioning software such as Otter.ai, which integrates with Zoom to provide live closed-captioning as well as meeting transcripts.

Host inclusive in-person events

Events are powerful spaces to bring people together—potentially from around the globe—to connect, share ideas, celebrate, and innovate. They are also spaces that may be ripe for exclusion and catering towards one group of people.

The message you signal about diversity and inclusion to your attendees is crucial to creating an impactful experience. You can set a precedent by thoughtfully considering the ways all attendees can feel embraced. Here's a checklist of best practices:

- Check cultural and faith calendars to ensure that mandatory organization events do not conflict with important holidays or dates.
- Use diverse suppliers whenever possible. This includes everything from transportation providers to sources of promotional products or event caterers.
- Create an inclusion statement/code of conduct that explicitly welcomes everyone and prohibits harassment and discrimination. Establish a zero-tolerance policy for homophobic, racist,

sexist, or any other biased language at your events. Publicize this on your website and during the event. Also, clearly communicate your stance and expectations to your team, attendees, sponsors, and vendors.

- Seek to integrate art and music from a variety of different cultural backgrounds.
- Include images of all kinds of people in conference marketing to promote diversity.
- Consider ways to engage the local community in the conference. Look for opportunities where participants can contribute to work occurring in the community as volunteers, not just as strictly tourists.
- Ensure a variety of food to meet people's cultural, religious, and dietary needs.
- Consider integrating real-time reflection moments. Examples include: integrated minutes of silence, moments in between presentations where participants are invited to journal or think about how what they've heard applies to them, guided breath or meditation moments, etc.
- Establish a childcare room that allows parents to come and go.
- Provide private breastfeeding rooms for nursing mothers.
- Provide prayer rooms.
- Work with Business Resource Groups to organize meet-ups during the conference to encourage a greater sense of community at the event.
- Provide buttons or ribbons for name badges so people can self-identify as anything they want! At registration, include buttons with terms like introvert, vegetarian, gamer, theatre nerd, etc. Also include opportunities for pronoun sharing. Not only will these pins provide useful conversation starters in intimidating rooms of strangers, they will also allow attendees to feel more authentically themselves.

Whatever policies you decide on, be sure to clearly communicate to attendees what they should expect at the event. Communicate details such as the menu, venue, bathroom accommodations, transportation, etc., so guests can have an understanding of what arrangements have been made ahead of time.

Deep Dive:

LGBTQ+ INCLUSION AT LIVE EVENTS.

Look for LGBTQ+ friendly destinations. As of the time of writing, LGBTQ+ discrimination is legal in 28 U.S. states with many popular event destinations. Note that individual counties and cities may have their own inclusive protections. Before choosing a destination, visit LGBTMap.org to see whether that location has LGBTQ+ protections. Have an honest conversation with any contact at the Convention and Visitors Association (CVA) about these concerns.[202]

If you're considering an event location that doesn't have LGBTQ+ inclusive protections, tell your CVA and venue contacts that discrimination is unacceptable. Ask the venue whether their staff have received LGBTQ+ inclusive diversity training.

Train your attendee-facing employees on transgender-inclusion. Train them so there are no embarrassing incidents like an attendee being misgendered. Remove gendered language such as "sir" and "ma'am" from your standard greetings.

Include pronoun identification. As part of the event registration process, show pronouns on name badges or offer them on stickers at the registration desk. Many organizations now give attendees the option to add pronoun labels to their name badges, or collect pronouns during the online registration process, and then print the pronouns directly on the badges.

Provide diverse gender options on forms. Update your registration and other forms to include 'Other' as a third gender option, and offer gender-neutral honorifics (such as Mx.). When folks self-identify using "Other" as a gender option and/or select an honorific such as "Mx.," your service to these attendees will be elevated because you can address them properly.

Create all-gender restrooms. Create a policy that allow attendees to choose the restroom of their actual gender identity and create at least one all-gender restroom in the event space. This could be as simple as rebranding a single-stall restroom for "All-genders." For an even bolder approach, rebrand multi-stall restrooms for all-genders. Then, make sure your team is prepared to direct attendees appropriately and explain the policy.

Include LGBTQ+ leaders. Whether it's through your program, host committee, marketing collateral, registration mailer, or keynote speaker, the LGBTQ+ people in your company should have a platform at your event. Simply bringing in an openly LGBTQ+ speaker to speak on sales is a powerful way to be inclusive.

Ditch the "Ladies and Gentlemen!" Speaking of speakers, encourage your speakers, emcees, and hosts to ditch the "Ladies and Gentlemen!" and instead use phrases like "Distinguished guests." That gendered phrase excludes folks who identify outside of the gender binary.

Include remote employees

The year 2020 forced organizations to face many tough questions such as:

How do we best engage our now-remote employees?

How do we get maximum productivity while creating inclusive spaces for people working remotely?

As the pandemic stretched on, organizations realized that employees may have been feeling isolated from their families, friends, and teams. Organizations looked for solutions to keep employees safe but also energized and connected to each other.

Because the office is typically a physical barrier between work and home, employees may struggle with boundaries and work longer hours. They may work through what could typically be commute time. Be mindful of this potential for burnout and encourage your team to take breaks. Also remind your team of any organizational counseling or wellness benefits that can help them promote personal health if your organization provides those services.

Most of all, be empathetic if people can't give 100%, 100% of the time. Everyone's home office setup is unique and not always ideal. You may have employees still working from their dining room tables with frequent interruptions from kids and pets. Give them grace.

Don't forget that for many employees, the workplace is a social outlet. A great workplace culture can give employees a true sense of belonging. According to Coqual, 40% of employees report feeling isolated at work. High belonging was linked to a 56% increase in job performance, a 50% drop in turnover risk, and a 75% reduction in sick days. This would result in annual savings of more than $52 million for an organization with 10,000 employees.[203]

Remote work doesn't appear to be going away any time soon. In fact, Twitter told most of its employees that they can work remotely forever. I believe that we'll see many more organizations doing the same going forward.[204]

Here are some tips to keep your team remotely socialized:

- Share articles and general life updates with your teams.
- Schedule one-on-ones and office hours to create a space for employees to connect with each other outside of work and understand how they are coping with the significant changes to our world.
- Leverage virtual meeting technology for virtual workshops to promote well-being and self-care. This can be done by setting aside time for team guided meditation or yoga, virtual "water cooler" chats, trivia nights, online games, etc.
- Create interest group channels for employees to form a connection with their peers (pets, gardening, film/tv, books, etc.)
- Continue to celebrate accomplishments, birthdays, anniversaries, and everything else with each other! If budget permits, send your employees gifts for these milestones.

Design inclusive products and services

When teams look alike and have similar backgrounds, they lose perspective. They generally see things in similar ways. Essentially, they have tunnel vision. When teams lose perspective, they don't see the full picture and often miss ways to be inclusive. This could mean that products fail to consider the needs of people with disabilities. It could mean that products fail to consider their audience and what sensitivities that audience has. It could mean that a lot of people get offended—like those H&M customers I mentioned earlier.

Diversity matters. But it has to be authentic.

There are many organizations that deeply care about creating inclusive products and experiences. Let's dig into some of their creative ideas.

Riv's Toms River Hub, a New Jersey restaurant, has a specific sensory dining room that caters to children with autism. This sensory dining room, called Chase's Friends Zone, has soothing lighting, a visual menu, and trained servers to make the dining experience as inclusive as possible. It even has a private entrance. All of the waiters have been certified by the organization KultureCity, which trains people on autism-inclusion. [204]

Not only that, but the restaurant donates 20% of its proceeds from meals in this room to an organization that supports people with autism.

Monica Hmielewski is a member of the family who owns the restaurant and mother to Chase, the young boy who inspired the idea. She said, *"I've talked to many people who haven't been out to eat for years. People are literally stopping me now to say, 'I can't thank you enough.'"* [205]

Target now offers adaptive costumes for kids with disabilities or sensory issues. Several of the costumes are designed specifically for wheelchair users, including a dragon, robot, pirate ship, and a royal carriage. Meanwhile, costumes such as the shark and unicorn are designed for kids with sensory concerns. Those costumes include features such as flat seams, no tags, and hidden openings. [206]

The beloved card game UNO also became a bit more inclusive. In 2019, Mattel announced that UNO cards will now be available in braille. *"With the launch of UNO Braille, we're making a real impact on a community that has been underserved by providing a game that both blind and sighted people can play together,"* said Ray Adler, Global Head of Games at Mattel in a press release.[207]

The packaging is not only in braille, but braille is on the corners of each card in the 112-card deck, to identify the card's color and number action.

Google revealed that they have 2,000 employees solely focused on creating inclusive products. These employees are embedded in project teams to ensure they are building tools for everyone. The idea is to address bias from the start and visit all types of communities to assess the wide variety of digital needs.

Google has trained 12,000 technical engineers on **inclusive design** and how to bring it into their goals. The engineers are asked to be aware of the different factors that affect how someone may interact with Google products. These could include ethnicity, gender, age, culture, ability level, socioeconomic level, and more.

These employees ask the right questions when products are designed. *"Have we talked to international users, have we talked to older users, have we talked to someone with a vision impairment?"* Annie Jean Baptiste, Google's head of product inclusion, asked.[208]

It's important to note that if the Google team catches a product that's not inclusive, they may not have the power to stop its launch. But those teams do make corrections when they find areas of opportunity—and you can do the same. Even if you don't catch that a product is not inclusive until it's in the market, you can take steps to fix the mistake.

Comcast Xfinity became the first company in the cable industry to offer customer service and technical support available in the fourth most used language in the U.S.—American Sign Language. They partnered with Connect Direct and offered support through an ASL call center program designed by the Communication Service for the Deaf (CSD).

David L. Cohen, former Senior Executive Vice President and Chief Diversity Officer at Comcast Corporation said, *"By partnering with Connect Direct and working with the deaf community, we want to address and break down the barriers to broadband adoption that are unique to this population. That starts by being able to speak with customers in their native language."* [209]

Even the ride-sharing apps, Uber and Lyft, will teach you sign language if your driver is deaf or hearing-impaired. When that's the case, riders will receive a notification and can learn things like "Hello" and "Thank You," or spell out their name. Then they'll be given a GIF with the word(s) in ASL. Pretty nifty and an easy way to breakdown a language barrier.[210]

Mastercard announced a new policy in 2019 to be inclusive of transgender and non-binary folks whose chosen name may not be reflected on their photo identification and debit card. This program, called True Name, debuted with BMO Harris Bank and has since rolled out to other banks. [211]

Applicants for the card must apply using their legal name to verify the customer's identity. But the name on the debit or ATM card does not have to be the holder's legal name. Their legal name remains on the account but customers can request a card with their preferred name. There's no requirement for anyone to identify themselves as transgender, gender non-conforming, or non-binary, or to specify a reason they want a True Name card.

As your organization considers new products, be sure to look at the process through an inclusive lens: does your product truly include everyone?

Inclusive 360 Action Steps

☐ Update your restroom and other facilities to be transgender-inclusive.

☐ Create policies to ensure your in-person events are inclusive of LGBTQ+ people and other marginalized people.

☐ Provide managers with a guide to host inclusive remote meetings.

☐ Explore your products and services and create an inclusion checklist as part of all new product development.

☐ Look into previous and/or current products and services and see what other ways you can be inclusive.

Keep learning:

- Book: Building For Everyone by Annie Jean-Baptiste
- LGBT Meeting Professionals Association: www.lgbtmpa.com

CHAPTER 14

Voices Carry
Allyship

Use your words

ALLYSHIP CAN TAKE MANY FORMS. An ally is your voice when you're not in the room—or even when you are in the room and don't feel safe enough to speak up! We all need allies, but underrepresented folks need them the most. It's not always easy for allies to find the right words, although, in my observation, younger generations feel greater freedom to express themselves.

My 10-year-old son is not shy about telling me how he feels. He's also not shy about telling others what's up. Two years ago, we were at a playground and he was playing with some unfamiliar kids when I overheard him telling his new friends that I'm not his real mommy.

Sigh.

The backstory is that my son Patrick has two moms, but only one of them (not me) gave birth to him. The science of this all can be a bit confusing to a young kid, so I sat him down for the talk about how we're both his real mommy, even though only one of us gave birth to him. But my point here is that Patrick, like many young kids, has been taught since the day he learned to talk to "use your words." He's been told that when he's having a tantrum. He's been told that when he's crying for some unknown reason. He's been told that over and over and over again: "It's OK, honey. Use your words."

Apparently, this messaging turned Patrick into an over-sharer.

When this message is used *against* me, like at the playground, I have to remind Patrick, "I'm so glad you're using your words—but some topics are best left for family discussion only!"

Still, I'm so glad that Patrick has been taught by us, by teachers, and by other adults that it's OK to talk about your feelings. He and other kids are learning about emotions in a way that I didn't learn about until much later. There are plenty of children's books written specifically to teach kids that feelings are normal, valid, and part of our humanity.

Patrick and many other kids his age are being taught that it's not only OK, but great to talk about your feelings. It's important. It's healthy. We're not mind readers.

That's certainly not how I was raised. My parents were immigrants from Ireland, and I was taught not by words, but by actions, to buck up.

Toughen up.
Get over it.
Suck it up.
Don't complain.
Just be grateful.

And

We don't talk about that with anyone.

These are not necessarily bad messages, but they reinforce the belief that we should simply move on, ignore, and avoid conflict and our own emotions.

I have first cousins who live in a small town with a population of 2,000. They are both kind, generous men in their 40s, and they haven't spoken to each other in at least 10 years—even as both their parents have been moved to nursing homes. Even as they have buried aunts and uncles. Who knows what the fight was about? They might not remember themselves.

When my siblings and I visit that town, the whole family goes out to the pub along with my cousins. The cousins don't speak, despite being mere steps from each other. Perhaps to them, it's not even awkward anymore. For us, it certainly is.

In my family, we were brilliant at the coping mechanism of "avoidance." Maybe you can relate. What conversations are you avoiding?

The problem with avoidance is that it creates additional stress and anxiety while we bury our thoughts and feelings just to minimize conflict, just to fly under the radar or go unnoticed. In the workplace, avoidance is a common coping mechanism. This can especially play out when faced with blurred lines. *Avoid the bully. Avoid the person who makes you uncomfortable. Avoid the Black person whom you don't know how to reach out to after the latest traumatic racial incident. Avoid the transgender person whose pronouns you may mess up.*

Avoid. Avoid. Avoid.

But when we avoid, we miss out on opportunities to understand others. We miss out on opportunities for professional growth. And we miss out on the opportunity to fulfill our potential. Life is smaller when we ignore experiences rather than challenge ourselves and communicate, even when it's hard.

I challenge you not to avoid but to approach. Approaching does not require conflict. Approaching can be casual or it can be stern, or it can even be silly.

If you find yourself in a situation where you overhear something offensive, where you feel uncomfortable and want the discussion to stop, *use your words.*

Allyship can be an individual act of acknowledging one's own privilege, as National Basketball League player Kyle Corver (now retired) did in the essay "Privileged," which he wrote for the *Player's Tribune.* Corver takes the readers on a journey from his lack of awareness to acknowledging his advantages and privilege.

In the essay, Corver challenged himself to become "part of the solution" against racism. He described some bias incidents he witnessed against Black teammates and admitted his inaction: *"I know that, as a white man, I have to hold my fellow white men accountable."* [212]

Corver's essay led to a closed-door team meeting/listening session with the president of the Utah Jazz, during which his Black teammates shared stories of degrading experiences they had simply because of their race.

We simply have to talk (and listen) about challenging conversations and topics that we've been avoiding, and when the people with the most power (usually white people) speak up as allies, others listen.

If you're like me, you may be afraid of saying the wrong thing. For years, I was terrified of saying something insensitive about race. So, I said nothing. Any time I was invited to a Black Lives Matter rally near me, or to a fundraiser for inner city kids, I'd be like "I have my thing... I do the gay thing...that's my thing...." I stayed quiet in my little gay lane.

Have you ever stayed exclusively in your lane, whatever your lane happens to be?

I hear from others that they're afraid of messing up the LGBTQ+ letters or terms. So, they say nothing. We are often more afraid of embarrassing ourselves than we are eager to connect with others.

What I now know is that staying in my lane kept my world smaller. And I know that the solution is much simpler than I realized—I simply had to be more curious. I simply had to follow the ARC.

The ARC Method® can also be used in any situation in which you are looking for clarity.

Remember, it's always better to ask, rather than assume.

In the workplace, let's say you have a coworker named Alex who is a single parent balancing work and a child with a disability. Alex has missed some team deadlines.

Let's take this situation through the ARC. Again, as with the other ARC examples, context and tone matter! Approach with curiosity, not confrontation!

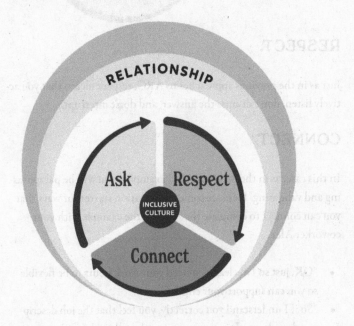

ASK.

In this situation, you are asking questions of Alex. Here are some sample ways to ask for more clarity:

- "How are you feeling today in two words?"
- "Can you tell me how I can best support you so we finish this project on time?"
- "Can you help me help you so we stay on track? What do you need from me?"

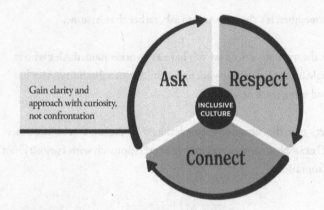

RESPECT.

Just as in the previous approaches to ARC, respect means that you actively listen, don't dismiss the answer, and don't interrupt.

CONNECT.

In this case, as in the previous ARC examples, you will be paraphrasing and validating. Here are some conversation starters or ways that you can connect to complete the ARC in the example with your coworker Alex.

- "OK, just so I'm clear, you need your work hours to be flexible so you can support your child. Got it!"
- "So if I understand you correctly, you feel that the job description has changed since you came on board, and there's too much on your plate. Understood. Thanks for bringing this to me. I'll work on this."

Then MOVE ON! No need to drag out the conversation, although if you need more clarity, go for another round of the ARC. Continue to use the ARC Method® until you feel like you have the clarity you need to move forward positively.

Remember, if you fail to follow any steps of the ARC, the ARC will fall flat and the status quo will remain.

Speak out against microaggressions

Microaggressions are subtle acts of exclusion that marginalize others. They can be verbal or nonverbal. They may take the form of slights, snubs, or insults. They may be intentional or unintentional, but ultimately communicate hostile, derogatory, or negative messages to others based on their part in a marginalized group.

Microaggressions could show up in the form of backwards compliments such as, "You are so articulate" (said to a BIPOC), or they could be an offhanded joke like, "That's so gay!" They can even attempt to violate someone physically, such as something many Black women report: "Can I touch your hair?"

Another common microaggression is white people calling BIPOC by the name of a different BIPOC person, or mispronouncing names altogether with no attempt to do better. A friend shared the following story with me:

Employees that I have worked with for many years can't tell the difference between me and a co-worker, and get us confused, even though individually I have shared details of my life with a person and I have listened to theirs. This other employee and I have different personalities, different body shapes, we speak differently... literally everything about us is different except our skin tone and hair. All this time that I've been getting to know someone I've been reduced down to skin and hairstyle.

Microaggressions can even happen in a remote-working world. Folks report hearing comments like, "Could whomever that is with the kid noise go on mute?" Or "What's that weird thing behind you?"

While microaggressions may be micro compared to violence, hate crimes, and overt -isms (racism, sexism, etc.), folks with marginalized identities report much higher incidences of microaggressions than others. These microaggressions contribute to a psychologically unsafe work environment, which contributes to a host of other problems. Microaggressions lead to lack of trust, lack of productivity, and employee turnover, to name a few. [213]

If you happen to overhear a comment that you feel is harassing, potentially harassing, borderline offensive, or any other form of microaggression, it's important to speak up as an ally. It's a key part of allyship. But how do you speak up when you witness such a thing? Follow the ARC.

Let's use a real-world example of a microaggression that you may overhear at work: "LGBTQ? What's the Q? And what's next, X, Y, and Z?"

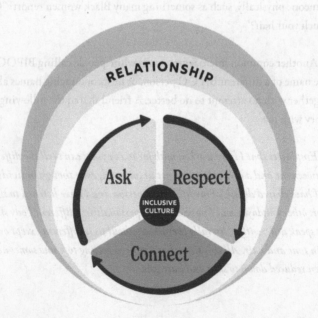

ASK.

Again, ask from a place of curiosity. In some cases, even start with a compliment such as, "I've always thought of you as a thoughtful person..."

Allies ask good questions when they follow the ARC, and context matters. The way you approach the conversation may depend on your relationship with the person—perhaps you may choose to pull the person aside to follow the ARC privately. Perhaps, if someone is half-joking or says, "I'm just joking!" you can approach them with a joking-back tone. To be successful with ARC, the place matters and your tone matters.

Here are some conversation starters for the Ask using the example above:

- "The Q means Queer, which used to be hurtful but is now an umbrella term—but can you explain what you meant by 'X, Y, and Z'? I'm super confused!"
- "Did I hear you correctly when you said X, Y, and Z? That would be weird!?"
- "Do you mind if we talk about your LGBTQ X, Y, Z comment? I don't get it."
- "Did you mean to say LGBTQXYZ? I may have misunderstood."

Again, stay in the space of curiosity, not confrontation.

These questions challenge the person to explain themselves and possibly realize how silly and/or offensive they may have been.

RESPECT.

As they explain themselves, follow up with the R—Respect. Simply put, respecting means being an active listener.

Keep your arms uncrossed, nod your head, and use verbal cues to indicate that you're paying attention. Don't dismiss what the other person is saying. Respectfully listen without interruption—even if you disagree! This may be hard. But you don't change behavior by ridicule or shame.

CONNECT.

Here are some ways to connect using the example above:

- "Ah yes, you're saying that the letters are confusing. That's what I used to think, too...."
- "OK, just so I'm clear, you don't really think there's an XYZ, just that there are so many letters? I get why you would say that but..."
- "So I understand you correctly, you think the letters are over-kill? I remember thinking that, but..."

Now, the other person may still get defensive or begin debating, in which case go back to the start of the ARC. This can be a cycle, and you can't expect to change "hearts and minds" with every person, but the ARC does have a powerful ability to "call someone out" and gently challenge them to reflect on their word choice.

Language is a powerful tool in creating an environment that welcomes everyone and establishes a common understanding. Language has the incredible power to include—and exclude.

Deep Dive:

YOUR OWN MICROAGGRESSIONS

But what if someone approaches me about my own microaggressions?

If you find yourself in a situation where someone has approached you with a concern, remember your intention does not always equal the impact that's been experienced by the other party. Here are some ways to handle it:

- Listen to the concerns. Attempt to understand the impact you made. Avoid common responses like, "I didn't mean it!" which can invalidate the other person's experience. Avoid the all-too-common "I was just joking!" which can be perceived as making light of someone else's pain.
- Verbally validate that their feelings are valid. It's fair to share that it wasn't your intention, but you understand that you created a negative impact.
- Apologize, but accept that it's OK if you're not forgiven. Don't make it about you!
- Most importantly, try to let it go and move on. We're all human and we make mistakes. Don't turn this into a big production where the person you slighted then feels responsible to take care of you.

Use inclusive language

Historically, language has been frequently used to exclude others. Lawmakers have used language to discriminate against groups because of their race, gender, sexual orientation, and more. Organizations have used language to exclude employees, even inadvertently, through things like gendered bathroom signs. And of course, people use language to exclude each other via microaggressions and slurs.

We can all do better. We can all be more respectful and impartial. We can all speak more inclusively to be better allies for one another.

This requires commitment. Language habits are deeply embedded. Many words and phrases have long gone unchallenged. It's possible you'll always feel like someone is judging what you say, even if your intentions are good. Unfortunately, communication is not only about what you say, but also how it's heard.

It takes time and constant work to change our habits. I still make mistakes. We all learn and move on, so please don't give up. If you make a mistake, acknowledge it, recommit to your goals, and move on. Here is some advice and key takeaways to keep in mind:

A key element of inclusive language is putting people first. Use the person-first phrase that puts the person ahead of their characteristics. For example, instead of "a disabled man" or "a female engineer," use "a man with a disability" or "a woman on our engineering team." People-first language prioritizes the person more than our descriptors.

Mention characteristics like gender, sexual orientation, religion, racial group, or ability only when relevant to the discussion. For example, there's usually no need to say, "Mike's the gay guy in accounting."

Avoid jargons and acronyms. These can exclude people who may not be on the "inside" and may not have the specialized language. Many jargons don't translate well from country to country, and some are based in stereotypes ("hold down the fort," and "call a spade a spade" are examples).

Avoid implying victimhood with phrases such as "afflicted by," "victim of," "suffers from," or "confined to a wheelchair."

Even euphemisms like "challenged," "differently abled," or "specially-abled," can be off-putting.

Avoid references to mental illness. Just because someone is fussy doesn't mean they have "OCD," a real disability. Just because someone can be moody doesn't mean they're "bipolar." Even "crazy" and "psycho" imply negative mental health.

Nobody is "normal," although they may be "typical." There's bias in using one group as a standard against which others are judged. Use of the word normal can stigmatize people who are different and imply they are abnormal.

Avoid gendered greetings. And yes, this means you shouldn't greet a group of people who appear to be women with "Hi ladies!" Terms like "ladies," "gals," or "girls" can feel patronizing to some. This also means that you should reprogram yourself from saying, "Hey guys!" to mixed-gender groups. I realize this is really, really hard, but the use of "guys" assumes that the default human is male. The use of guys, ladies, boys, girls, gentlemen, and any other gendered language terms also may exclude folks whose gender is outside the binary.

If you've noticed in this book, I'm a big fan of the gender-neutral term "folks." Hey folks. Yes, this works even if you're not in the South. "Everyone" works well also, as does "Y'all."

I realize old habits are hard to break, but here are a few more considerations:

SAY THIS	NOT THAT
Workforce, personnel, workers	Manpower, man hours
Chairperson, chair	Chairman
Spouses/partners	Wives, husbands, boy-friends, girlfriends
Parenting	Mother, fathering
Underrepresented groups, marginalized groups	Minorities

When (not if, because it does happen) you mess up, keep it simple and don't over-apologize. Say your version of "You're right. I apologize for not understanding what that word meant to you. I'm going to work on this and be better."

Then move on. We're all learning and growing and trying to be better allies.

One word that seems to be particularly vexing for folks is the singular pronoun *they*, frequently used by non-binary folks.

Citing a 313% increase in searches for this word, Merriam Webster Dictionary declared the singular "they" as Word of the Year in 2019. This is what Merriam-Webster wrote:

"Our Word of the Year for 2019 is they. It reflects a surprising fact: even a basic term—a personal pronoun—can rise to the top of our data. Although our lookups are often driven by events in the news, the dictionary is also a primary resource for information about language itself, and the shifting use of they has been the subject of increasing study and commentary in recent years." [214]

Similarly, the American Psychological Association updated its Bias-Free Language Guide to embrace the use of the singular "they" to refer to people whose gender is non-binary, and/or unknown or irrelevant. This makes the singular "they" officially good practice in scholarly writing and in everyday speaking and writing, which means we should all do it.

The guide states:

"When referring to individuals whose identified pronouns are not known or when the gender of a generic or hypothetical person is irrelevant within the context, use the singular "they" to avoid making assumptions about an individual's gender. Use the forms "they," "them," "theirs," and so forth.

Sexist bias can occur when pronouns are used carelessly, as when the pronoun "he" is used to refer to all people, when a gendered pronoun is used exclusively to define roles by sex (e.g., "the nurse . . . she"), or when "he" and "she" are alternated as though these terms are generic. Pronouns associated with a specific gender have been found to induce readers to think of individuals of that gender even when the pronoun use is intended to be generic."[215]

Still not convinced?

The Oxford English Dictionary traces first use of the singular "they" all the way back to 1375. It's been used in writing by William Shakespeare, Emily Dickinson, and William Wadsworth Longfellow.[216]

In general, remember that language is ever-evolving. Dictionaries now include new-ish terms such as screen time, unplug (referencing going off of screen time), gig economy, and chai latte.

Be an organizational ally

Allyship is not just an individual behavior. Organizations can be allies, too, by being advocates for inclusive policies and speaking up in defense of marginalized groups. I've made mention to several organizations throughout this book that have begun to do this more regularly, particularly around issues of LGBTQ+ inclusion and racial justice.

The restaurant Cracker Barrel used to have a reputation as a company that allowed racial and anti-LGBTQ+ discrimination, even as recently as 2004. They have turned around in big ways, not only in their inclusion strategies, but also with a 325% increase in stock prices, under the leadership of their CEO Sandra Cochran.

In 2019, Cracker Barrel clearly denounced LGBTQ+ discrimination, issuing a statement about why it banned anti-LGBTQ+ Pastor Grayson Fritts from hosting meetings in their restaurant:

"At Cracker Barrel, we work hard to foster a culture that is welcoming and inclusive—we have a zero-tolerance policy for discriminatory treatment or harassment of any sort," the release read. *"We take pride in serving as a home away from home for all guests and in showing our communities and our country that the hospitality we practice is open to everyone."*

"We believe it's crucially important to foster this environment for our employees for many reasons," former Cracker Barrel spokeswoman Janella Escobar told the Knoxville News Sentinel. *"The guest experience should never exceed the employee experience, because our success begins with the employee experience. Happy employees create happy guests,"* she added. *"We want our employee community to reflect the diversity of the communities we serve."* [217]

That is allyship in action. Although the restaurant received flak on social media for selling out to political correctness, it's made many more new fans.

Similarly, as I wrote in Chapter 6, many organizations spoke out against racism in the aftermath of George Floyd's murder in 2020. CEO Bill Penzey of Penzey's Spices took it a step further. Jacob Blake, another Black man, was shot by police in Kenosha, Wisconsin, 50 miles from the headquarters of Penzey's Spices. The aftermath of that shooting included some rioting and looting in the area.

CEO Penzey, who publicly supports Black Lives Matter, responded to a comment from a customer saying, *"You would be singing a different tune if it was your store being looted [by the protestors]."*

Penzey's response was, *"Human life means everything; stuff, not so much."* Then he announced plans to "loot" his own store in Kenosha. Penzey's gave that store's equivalent of spices and gift boxes to food pantries and organizations working on social justice. Bill Penzey walked the talk. He used his voice and influence to speak out against injustice. Pretty cool. That's also allyship in action and an action a lot of organizations can learn from.[218]

Open to All is a program from the LGBT Movement Advancement Project and is designed to help the LGBTQ+ community know which businesses to trust. Yelp allows business owners to designate themselves as "Open to All" on their business dashboard, and this is now a searchable feature within the review site. [219]

Tapestry Inc (which owns Coach, Kate Spade, and many other brands) and Gap Inc. are among the retailers to sign the Open to All pledge to demonstrate LGBTQ+ inclusion. These companies and others that sign the pledge receive a sticker to use on all of their storefronts across North America.

If your organization has a storefront, join the Open to All campaign to demonstrate your allyship—but don't forget to train your employees on LGBTQ+ inclusive customer service so they live up to the promise you're making as part of that campaign.

Recover from mistakes

On your organization's DEI journey, you're going to make mistakes.

Starbucks Coffee ✓
@Starbucks

Follow

We apologize to the two individuals and our customers for what took place at our Philadelphia store on Thursday.

> We apologize to the two individuals and our customers and are disappointed this led to an arrest. We take these matters seriously and clearly have more work to do when it comes to how we handle incidents in our stores. We are reviewing our policies and will continue to engage with the community and the police department to try to ensure these types of situations never happen in any of our stores.

Earlier in the book, I wrote about Starbucks' racial bias incident in Philadelphia. There are always lessons to learn from incidents like this, and the teachable moment here is how Starbucks recovered.

Although Starbucks' initial apology was widely panned as weak, their CEO later made two subsequent apologies and personally traveled to Philadelphia to meet with the gentlemen who were arrested.

Just five days after the incident, Starbucks announced that all 8,000 corporate stores in the U.S. would close for a half-day mandatory racial bias training, which then became part of new employee onboarding.[220]

Starbucks apologized with sincerity, humility, and curiosity. They made specific, long-term commitments. And they got back to business.

Not surprisingly, their quick recovery caused their stock to remain relatively stable since the incident. All of the stores I walked by in the days since were as busy as ever.

If you find yourself or your organization in a situation where you have to recover from bias or a mistaken assumption, follow Starbucks' lead. First, apologize sincerely and admit you made a mistake. Next, become curious to explore why this happened. In this case, Starbucks realized that their partners are susceptible to unconscious bias. Finally, connect the information you found to real systemic change—like the training that is now part of all new employee onboarding at Starbucks.

Like Starbucks, you will make mistakes on this journey. They're inevitable, but we're all in this together, and we're all going to make mistakes. Be patient with yourself, and be patient with each other. Keep moving forward.

Inclusive 360 Action Steps

- ☐ Use your voice and speak out against injustices and microaggressions that you witness.
- ☐ If you have a storefront, join the Open to All campaign.
- ☐ Be aware of other opportunities to speak out as an organizational ally.

Keep learning:

- Newsletter: 5 Ally Actions www.betterallies.com
- Book: What If I Say the Wrong Thing by Verna A. Myers
- Book: Lead Like an Ally by Julie Kratz
- Book: Subtle Acts of Exclusion by Tiffany Jana and Michael Baran
- Book: You'll Never Believe What Happened to Lacey by Amber Ruffin and Lacey Lamar

EPILOGUE

Don't Stop Believin'
Understanding Belonging

WHEN YOUR ORGANIZATION changes its policies and uses extensive training to build empathy, curiosity, and psychological safety, it's on its way to the holy grail: belonging.

The Oxford English Dictionary defines belonging as: *the feeling of being comfortable and happy in a particular situation or with a particular group of people.*

Belonging is about having our most fundamental human needs met—the need to connect and be a part of something bigger than ourselves. It's about being loved and having a sense of purpose. It's about using our words and having them listened to. Belonging is about having a sense of community and a sense of unity.

In the workplace, belonging is kind of like the opposite of covering, which I wrote about in Chapter 11. To belong at work is to be authentic and wholly expressed. It means that you are valued and loved for your differences, not in spite of them. To create a sense of belonging at work, every leader and every manager must be able to articulate just how much every person matters. The organization's goals are not enough. Belonging requires people-first leadership.

And of course, when an employee feels like they belong in their organization, they're going to do their best work. They're going to go the extra mile, feel generous with their ideas, express their creativity, and be curious and empathetic about others. Many organizations are even now calling their DEI department their DIB (Diversity, Inclusion, and Belonging) or DEIB (Diversity, Equity, Inclusion, and Belonging) department.

You can also create a sense of belonging among your customers. That often comes from an organization who lives its purpose, from an organization that leads with its WHY. Read more about that in Simon Sinek's great book *Start with Why*. Combine a strong sense of purpose with great DEI and corporate social responsibility, and you'll build belonging (and loyalty) with your customers.

Belonging is not a fixed state. It's a process, and it must be nurtured—because it doesn't take much for employees to suddenly feel unsafe, to feel like they don't belong. Any employee can lose a sense of belonging after a series of microaggressions or feeling deeply let down by leaders. Any employee can stop feeling like they belong the second they feel excluded.

Belonging is aspirational, in a way. It takes significant effort. There is no magic formula to establish belonging.

If I were to write a recipe, though, it would look something like this:

Change or implement 20 policies, using ideas from throughout this book, ideally from each chapter so you have a balanced approach!

+ Inclusive Leadership training and coaching for all managers and leaders

+ Ongoing allyship workshops for all individual contributors

+ DEI metrics in all employee assessments

+ New inclusive norms for all events

+ Inclusion checklists used in marketing

+ Inclusion checklists used in product design

But the truth is that belonging is somewhat intangible. You can attempt to measure it with inclusion surveys and your balance sheet, but there's something about belonging that's almost *magic*.

You know what's really cool? You have the ability to create that magic.

You *(yes, you!)* can help those who have fewer advantages than you feel like they belong. You can step up as a mentor or a sponsor. You can intentionally provide access to spending opportunities. You can offer access to the systems that you influence or control. Take action and start with one person or one business.

It feels really, *really* good to offer access and opportunities to those who have fewer. I know….I have my own business and actively do this work internally.

Remember, this work takes time. All of the ideas in this book are meant to work together but they each take time. And if you're like me and not a process-oriented person, you're going to need to tap into that "why" over and over again. Nothing is ever a quick fix, and it will take time to see real change, but it's always worth it.

Trust the ARC as you do this work. When you find yourself at a loss for words or actions, start by asking a great question. Respect the answers you find and then connect to real solutions, to meaningful accountability.

The ARC Method® is about fulfilling your promise of building an organization that is *Inclusive 360.* Use it over and over again on your journey towards creating a culture of belonging.

We all deserve to belong. Every last person your organization touches: from the Chair of the Board to the customer who uses your product.

As poet Amanda Gorman declared in her poem at the 2021 U.S. presidential inauguration:

> *"For there is always light*
> *If only we are brave enough to see*
> *If only we're brave enough to be it."* [221]

Will you commit to being *Inclusive 360*? Will you be that light?

Book Club Discussion Questions

INCLUSIVE 360 WAS written to start meaningful conversations and get people in action towards greater diversity, equity, and inclusion. Here are some conversation starters and discussion questions that you can bring to your group.

- What does diversity mean to you? What's your own story of diversity?

- How is diversity discussed in your personal networks?

- How diverse are your personal networks? Your professional networks?

- How is diversity discussed at work?

- What mistaken assumptions have people made about you? How did it feel? What mistaken assumptions have you made about others?

- What does the leadership of your organization look like? Why do you think that is?

- If you were to bring some of the ideas from this book to organizational leadership, what kind of response do you think you'll get? How might you prepare yourself for the conversation?

- How does your office/community currently celebrate diversity? Does it feel authentic? Is there active participation?

- If your organization starts to increase diversity, how would you expect underrepresented talent to be treated by others? What makes you say that?

- How has your race played a part in your lived experience? How does this impact your sense of inclusion at work?

- What will you do to become an antiracist?

- What microaggressions have you witnessed in the past, especially at work? How did you respond, if at all? How did it feel to witness those microaggressions?

- What microaggressions have you experienced from others before? How did it feel?

- Do you personally feel a sense of belonging in your workplace? What contributes to that?

- What about the book is most applicable to you?

- Was there a section of the book that had the most impact on you? Share parts of that section and its impact.

- Did your opinions on the subject change due to the information contained in this book? Has your interest in the subject matter increased? How so?

- What questions do you still have after reading this book?

- What is one thing you can commit to doing as a result of having read this book?

Acknowledgments

These acknowledgments are about my journey of entrepreneurship and the magic that happens from saying yes to connecting. My journey began with my first business in 2004 as an activist LGBTQ+ wedding planner. I spent 14 years planning weddings but also training and consulting with businesses in the wedding, hospitality, and tourism industries. That work was formative, and I'm grateful for all of the couples who entrusted me with their stories.

Ultimately, it was time to evolve, and I'm grateful to my former coach Sunni VonMutius who said the magic words that challenged me to pivot my firm's focus beyond those industries and beyond LGBTQ+ specific work. Sunni also introduced me more to the world of "woo-woo" and a wide variety of tools I've since used to stay grounded and develop a healthier mindset–(especially as I battled severe imposter syndrome during my pivot / professional identity crisis!)

This entrepreneurial journey wouldn't be as much fun or as collaborative without a cheerleading squad. For years, I was always so independent, and proudly so–but over time, I've realized that I can go farther and have a lot more fun when I go with others.

My squad starts with my partner Heather Vickery, also an entrepreneur, who has been by my side through the exhilarating ride of entrepreneurship. Heather's a success coach, and I'm so grateful to be able to pull up a chair by her side and bounce ideas around or get feedback on a tough decision. I always feel cared for thanks to Heather's boundless wisdom, compassion, and generosity of spirit. I have a great time sitting around with her talking about our Enneagram score or books we've both read. I can't wait to see how our journeys continue to evolve. Together, we are both dream-makers.

A few years ago, Heather and I and some friends began an informal text group called "Team Life All Stars." We're all self-employed folks who challenge ourselves and believe in the power of our dreams–and we hold each other accountable to them. Thank you, Eddie Babbage,

Brooke Richie-Babbage, and Lisha McKoy. You're the greatest cheer-leaders. I love you all and am proud to be your friend.

I'm grateful to the many incredible people with whom I connected through my membership in the National LGBT Chamber of Commerce (and as a certified LGBT business enterprise). Thank you to my wonderful friends and sounding boards, Cindi Creager, Jenn T. Grace, Rhodes Perry, Tammi Wallace, and Jerome' Holston from the Illinois LGBT Chamber, for always thinking of me when opportunities arise.

As business started to grow, I put together a wonderful team. Thank you, Darnell Adams, Daniel Downer, Patti Flynn, October Gunawan, Rita Mays, Dr. Laura Quiros, and Erma Standley. You're so dependable and solid. You're the best.

Thank you to my pre-readers: Cathy Diorio, Katie Rasoul, Stefanie Robel, Jan Sugar, and Charlene Wheeless. Your feedback was incredibly helpful as I refined my message. Thank you to my editor, Brandi Lai, who made sure my message was clear and resonant. Thank you to Ian Berg, my very creative and patient book designer. A huge shout-out to Amber Villhauer and her team from NGNG Enterprises for pushing me way outside of my comfort zone as I brought this book into the world. You helped me build my tribe. Wow. That's magic.

Thank you to Jane Lee Kaddu for being my proofreader and best friend of 26 years. Thank you to Jen Gabriel, for your decades of friend-ship and beautiful foreword. I love you both!

Random, but to everyone in the "dead moms club": I see you, and I know how hard it is. Our moms are proud of us.

To all my fellow diversity, equity, and inclusion practitioners: stay the course. Wherever you are on your own journey, entrepreneur-ial or otherwise, keep planting seeds and keep showing up. The world needs you today.

Glossary

Asian American and Pacific Islander (AAPI): People of Asian, Asian American, or Pacific Islander ancestry.

Ableism: The assumption that there is an ideal body and mind that is better than all others. This leads to prejudiced thoughts and discriminatory actions based on differences in physical, mental, and/or emotional ability.

Accessibility: The degree a facility is readily approachable and usable by individuals with disabilities. Accessibility includes making spaces (including websites) and events accessible to people with physical disabilities, people who are neurodivergent, and people who may have different cognitive needs.

ADA: The Americans with Disabilities Act (ADA) is a U.S. civil rights law that prohibits discrimination against individuals with disabilities in all areas of public life, including jobs, schools, transportation, and all places that are open to the general public.

Ageism: Prejudice and discrimination against individuals or groups on the basis of their age.

Ally: Someone who supports a group other than their own (in terms of racial identity, gender, faith identity, sexual orientation, etc.) Allies acknowledge disadvantage and oppression of other groups; take risks and action on the behalf of others; and invest in strengthening their own knowledge and awareness of oppression.

Antiracism: The ongoing, proactive process of dismantling systems of racism and promoting racial equity.

Belonging: The feeling of being comfortable and happy in a particular situation or with a particular group of people.

Bias: Prejudice; an inclination or preference, especially one that interferes with impartial judgment.

Black, Indigenous, People of Color (BIPOC): An umbrella term that stands for Black, Indigenous, People of Color. This term can be used to describe anyone who identifies as a Black person, Indigenous person, or person of color. It is a term used to link the collective struggle for liberation and many shared experiences of racial injustice and discrimination experienced by BIPOC people.

Business Resource Groups: A group of people within an organization who choose to meet to explore a shared identity such as race, gender, age, religion, and sexual orientation. These may also be called Employee Resource Groups (ERGs), Employee Network Groups (ENGs), affinity groups, or similar terms

Cisgender: Individuals whose gender identity and expression line up with their birth-assigned sex.

Code switching: The practice of changing the way someone expresses themselves culturally and linguistically based on different parts of their identity.

Cover: The practice of hiding parts of ourselves to avoid stigmatization.

Diversity: Individual differences (ability, learning styles, and life experiences) and group/social differences (race/ethnicity, class, gender, sexual orientation, country of origin, as well as cultural, political, religious, or other affiliations) that can be engaged in the service of learning.

Equity: The practice of changing systems to make up for historical injustice and/or discrimination. Equity provides more for those who need it.

Gender identity: A person's perception of their gender, which may or may not correspond with their birth sex.

HBCU: An acronym that stands for "historically Black colleges and universities." These are institutions of higher education in the United States that were established with the intention of primarily serving the Black community, though they have always allowed admission to students of all races.

Inclusion: The state of creating spaces where everyone is a stakeholder. Inclusion enables individuals and groups to feel safe, respected, engaged, motivated, and valued for who they are and for their contributions toward organizational and societal goals.

Inclusive design: The process of making a product intuitive, accessible to, and usable by as many people as reasonably possible without the need for special adaptation or specialized design.

Intersectionality: The layers of marginalized identities that compound to create a more challenging lived experience for people with multiple marginalized identities. The term was coined by Kimberlé Crenshaw, who used it to describe the experiences of Black women—who experience both sexism and racism.

Latinx: A gender-neutral term often used in lieu of the gendered "Latino" or "Latina" when referring to individuals with cultural ties to Latin America and individuals of Latin American descent.

LGBTQIA: Acronym encompassing the diverse groups of lesbian, gay, bisexual, pansexual, transgender, queer, intersex, and asexual populations and allies/alliances/associations.

Marginalized identities/group: This term refers to people "on the margins," who have traditionally been excluded from economic, educational, and political systems typically due to their race, sexual orientation, gender identity, or other identities.

Microaggression: This term was coined by psychiatrist and Harvard University professor Chester M. Pierce in 1970 to describe the tiny, casual, almost imperceptible insults and degradation often felt by marginalized groups.

Neurodiversity: The idea that neurological differences like autism and ADHD are the result of normal, natural variation in the human genome.

Non-binary: Any gender identity that does not fit the male and female binary.

Queer: Historically a derogatory term towards gay people, this term has been reclaimed and is used as an umbrella term by many people who are not straight and/or cisgender.

Privilege: A right or advantage that only some people have access or availability to because of their social group membership.

Pronouns: A gender pronoun is a consciously chosen set of words that allows a person to accurately represent their gender identity. Some pronouns include she/her; he/him; and they/them. Non-binary people often use they/them as a singular pronoun.

Psychological safety: The belief that one will not be punished or humiliated for speaking up with ideas, questions, concerns or mistakes.

Sexual orientation: A term that describes whom a person feels romantically or sexually attracted to. Examples include straight, gay, bisexual, pansexual, bisexual, and asexual.

Sponsorship: A specific program where leaders use their influence to advance the careers of members of marginalized groups. Sponsors use their social capital and credibility to advocate for their sponsee by promoting, protecting, preparing, and supporting them.

Supplier diversity: Procurement programs designed to create more equity by expanding buying power to historically marginalized groups.

Transgender: Someone whose gender identity does not align with the gender they were assigned at birth. This is an umbrella term that also includes non-binary people. Someone who is transgender may or may not medically transition from male to female or female to male.

Unconscious/Implicit bias: The attitudes or stereotypes that affect people's understanding, actions, and decisions in an unconscious manner. These biases are activated involuntarily and without an individual's awareness or intentional control.

Underrepresented group: This term describes any subset of a population that holds a smaller percentage within a significant subgroup than it holds in the general population. Women and BIPOC are often underrepresented groups in science, technology, engineering, and mathematics, for example.

Notes

Introduction

[1] Wikimedia Foundation. (2021, April 14). *Day of Affirmation Address.*Wikipedia. en.wikipedia.org/wiki/Day_of_Affirmation_Address.

[2] *Search ADA.gov.* 2010 ADA regulations. www.ada.gov/2010_regs.htm.

[3] Spencer, E. (2019, January 13). *You'll Want To Pin This, Learnings From Pinterest's Diversity Successes.* Forbes. www.forbes.com/sites/erinspencer1/2018/09/11/transparency-at-pinterest-is-leading-to-a-more-diverse-team/?sh=1bd5acf73ee8.

CHAPTER 1
Walk this Way: Understanding Diversity

[4] Coqual. (2019, December 9). *Being Black in Corporate America: An Intersectional Exploration.* www.talentinnovation.org/_private/assets/BeingBlack-KeyFindings-CTI. pdf.

[5] Barta, T., Kleiner, M., & Neumann, T. (2018, February 16). *Is there a payoff from top-team diversity?* McKinsey & Company. www.mckinsey.com/business-functions/organization/our-insights/is-there-a-payoff-from-top-team-diversity.

[6] *Millennial Survey 2016: Deloitte: Social impact, Innovation.* (2017, May 9). www2.deloitte.com/al/en/pages/about-deloitte/articles/2016-millennialsurvey.html.

[7] *Over 86% of Job Seekers Say Workplace Diversity Is an Important Factor When Looking for a Job.* (2019, November 25). ZipRecruiter. www.prnewswire.com/news-releases/over-86-of-job-seekers-say-workplace-diversity-is-an-important-factor-when-looking-for-a-job-300964115.html.

[8] Allen, D. G. (2008). Society of Human Resources Management. *Retaining Talent: A Guide to Analyzing and Managing Employee Turnover.* www.shrm.org/hr-today/trends-and-forecasting/special-reports-and-expert-views/documents/retaining-talent. pdf.

[9] Scott, R. (2017, May 4). *Employee Engagement Vs. Employee Experience.* Forbes. www.forbes.com/sites/causeintegration/2017/05/04/employee-engagement-vs-employee-experience.

[10] Dixon-Fyle, S., Dolan, K., Hunt, V., & Prince, S. (2021, July 12). *Diversity wins: How inclusion matters.* McKinsey & Company. www.mckinsey.com/featured-insights/diversity-and-inclusion/diversity-wins-how-inclusion-matters.

[11] Hewlett, M.A., Marshall, M., & Sherbin, L. (2020, September 31). *Innovation, Diversity, and Market Growth.* Coqual. coqual.org/wp-content/uploads/2020/09/31_innovationdiversityandmarketgrowth_keyfindings-1.pdf

[12] *2020 Edelman Trust Barometer.* Edelman. www.edelman.com/trust/2020-trust-barometer.

[13] Hewlett, S., Marshall, M., and Sherbin, L. (2014, August 1). *How Diversity Can Drive Innovation.* Harvard Business Review. hbr.org/2013/12/how-diversity-can-drive-innovation.

[14] Edelman, Richard. (2019, August 20). *Business Into the Breach.* Edelman. www.edelman.com/insights/business-breach-roundtable

[15] Green, J. (2019, October 7). *Startups with Female Founders Raise More Venture Cash.* Bloomberg. www.bloomberg.com/news/articles/2019-10-07/startups-with-female-founders-raise-more-venture-cash.

[16] Green, J. (2020, January 21). *Hedge Funds Not Led By White Men Outperform Peers Nearly 2 to 1.* Bloomberg. www.bloomberg.com/news/articles/2020-01-21/hedge-funds-not-led-by-white-men-outperform-peers-nearly-2-to-1.

[17] McKeon, K. (2020, June 18). *How to Develop an Employer Branding Strategy in 2020.* The Manifest. themanifest.com/digital-marketing/employer-branding-strategy-2020.

[18] Economy, P. (2019, July 11). *Glassdoor Just Announced the Surprising Results of Its 2019 Mission and Culture Survey (How Does Your Company Stack Up?).* Inc.com. www.inc.com/peter-economy/glassdoor-just-announced-surprising-results-of-its-2019-mission-culture-survey-how-does-your-company-stack-up.html.

[19] *DEI Perspectives.* Deloitte United States. www2.deloitte.com/us/en/pages/about-deloitte/articles/inclusion-insights.html.

[20] Chamberlain, A. and Zhao, D. (2019, August 19). *The Key to Happy Customers?* Happy Employees. Harvard Business Review. hbr.org/2019/08/the-key-to-happy-customers-happy-employees.

CHAPTER 2:
Born this Way: Understanding Diversity

[21] Unleashed. www.theleadersguide.com/.

[22] www.law.columbia.edu/faculty/kimberle-w-crenshaw

[23] Mooney, C., & Viskontas, I. (2014, May 9). *The Science of Your Racist Brain.* Mother Jones. www.motherjones.com/politics/2014/05/inquiring-minds-david-amodio-your-brain-on-racism.

[24] Wible, P. (2016, October 20). *Her story went viral. But she is not the only black doctor ignored in an airplane emergency.* The Washington Post. www.washingtonpost.com/national/health-science/tamika-cross-is-not-the-only-black-doctor-ignored-in-an-airplane-emergency/2016/10/20/3f59ac08-9544-11e6-bc79-af1cd3d2984b_story.html.

[25] Fletcher, C. (2018, April 17). Bloomberg. *Starbucks Training Shutdown Could Cost Them Just 16.7 Million.* www.bloomberg.com/news/articles/2018-04-17/starbucks-training-shutdown-could-cost-them-just-16-7-million.

[26] Photos | Canva. www.canva.com/photos/.

[27] Hudson, C. Diversity (Part II): *Reversing Discriminatory Hiring Practices.* LinkedIn. www.linkedin.com/pulse/diversity-part-ii-reversing-discriminatory-hiring-carmen-hudson-csm.

[28] He, J. & Kaplan, S. G. (2019, July 29). *The debate about quotas. Gender and the Economy.* www.gendereconomy.org/the-debate-about-quotas.

[29] Settembre, J. *Delta Air Lines, Ralph Lauren among companies pledging to boost diversity in boardroom.* Yahoo!. www.yahoo.com/news/delta-air-lines-ralph-lauren-180058986.html.

[30] Tappe, A. (2019, October 21). *JPMorgan wants to hire people with criminal backgrounds.* CNN. www.cnn.com/2019/10/21/business/jpmorgan-criminal-record-jobs/index.html.

CHAPTER 3:
Formation: Increasing Diversity

[31] He, J. & Kaplan, S. G. (2019, July 29). *The debate about quotas*. Gender and the Economy. www.gendereconomy.org/the-debate-about-quotas.

[32] Matthews, C. (2014, November 3). *He Dropped One Letter On His Resume. Suddenly, Everyone Wanted Him*. HuffPost. www.huffpost.com/entry/jose-joe-job-discrimination_n_5753880.

[33] Prequin. (2018). *The Future of Alternatives*. docs.preqin.com/reports/Preqin-Future-of-Alternatives-Report-October-2018.pdf.

[34] Vozza, S. (2020, August 26). *This one decision helped an investment firm radically diversify its intern program*. Fast Company. www.fastcompany.com/90543477/this-one-decision-helped-an-investment-firm-radically-diversify-its-intern-program.

[35] HubSpot Careers. www.hubspot.com/careers.

[36] Morgan, C. (2017, July 12). *What We Learned from Improving Diversity Rates at Pinterest*. Harvard Business Review. hbr.org/2017/07/what-we-learned-from-improving-diversity-rates-at-pinterest.

[37] Thubron, R. (2015, August 5). *Intel doubles referral bonus for women and minority hires*. TechSpot. www.techspot.com/news/61645-intel-doubles-referral-bonus-women-en-minority-hires.html.

[38] Liu, J. (2020, October 6). *Former IBM CEO says employers should stop hiring based on college degrees and focus on this instead*. CNBC. www.cnbc.com/2020/10/02/former-ibm-ceo-ginni-rometty-hiring-based-on-skills-over-degree.html.

[39] Bariso, J. (2020, August 19). *Google Has Announced a Plan to Disrupt the College Degree. Inc.* www.inc.com/justin-bariso/google-plan-disrupt-college-degree-university-higher-education-certificate-project-management-data-analyst.html.

[40] Society of Human Resources Management. (2020, September 28). 8 *Diversity Recruiting Mistakes and How to Avoid Them*. www.shrm.org/resourcesandtools/hr-topics/talent-acquisition/pages/8-diversity-recruiting-mistakes-how-to-avoid-them.aspx

[41] Centers for Disease Control and Prevention. (2018, August 16). *CDC: 1 in 4 US adults live with a disability*. Centers for Disease Control and Prevention. www.cdc.gov/media/releases/2018/p0816-disability.html.

[42] Loubier, A. (2017, March 15). *How Working Remotely Is Helping Women Close The Gender Gap In Tech*. Forbes. www.forbes.com/sites/andrealoubier/2017/03/13/how-working-remotely-is-helping-women-close-the-gender-gap-in-tech.

[43] Smith, K. (2019, July 10). *Why remote work is inclusion work*. Abstract.com www.abstract.com/blog/remote-work-inclusion.

[44] Csreinicke. (2020, October 26). *It might be worth it to move to a cheaper city, even if your company cuts your pay*. CNBC. www.cnbc.com/2020/10/16/it-might-be-worth-it-to-move-during-the-pandemic-even-with-a-pay-cut-.html.

[45] MacLellan, L. *Spotify, Salesforce adopt "work from anywhere" policies*. Quartz. qz.com/work/1972103/spotify-salesforce-adopt-wfa-work-from-anywhere-policies.

[46] Society of Human Resources Management. *Employing Military Veterans Toolkit*. www.shrm.org/resourcesandtools/tools-and-samples/toolkits/pages/militaryreadyemployer.aspx

[47] *Bank of America Surpasses Five-Year Goal to Hire 10,000 Veterans*. Bank of America. newsroom.bankofamerica.com/press-releases/community/bank-america-surpasses-five-year-goal-hire-10000-veterans#.

[48] *Hilton Hires 30,000 U.S. Military Veterans Via Operation Opportunity.* Hilton. newsroom.hilton.com/corporate/news/hilton-hires-30000-us-military-veterans-via-operation-opportunity.

[49] Lagorio-Chafkin, C. (2018, May 22). *Chobani Founder Hamdi Ulukaya Says Hiring Refugees Isn't a Political Act.* Inc. www.inc.com/magazine/201806/christine-lagorio/chobani-yogurt-hamdi-ulukaya-hiring-refugees.html.

[50] *20 Global Companies Announce New Commitments to Help Address the Refugee Crisis.* The Tent Partnership for Refugees. www.tent.org/20-global-companies-announce-new-commitments-help-address-refugee-crisis.

[51] Knowledge, H. B. S. W. (2016, October 7). *The Benefits Of Recruiting Employees With Autism Spectrum Disorder.* Forbes. www.forbes.com/sites/hbsworkingknowledge/2016/07/11/the-benefits-of-recruiting-employees-with-autism-spectrum-disorder.

[52] Guardian News and Media. (2020, February 3). *Autism to ADHD: Thinking differently about recruitment.* The Guardian. www.theguardian.com/global/2020/feb/03/autism-to-adhd-thinking-differently-about-recruitment.

[53] *Why Dell Is Making Neurodiverse Hiring A Priority.* (2021, June 17). Catalyst. www.catalyst.org/2019/10/16/why-dell-is-making-neurodiverse-hiring-a-priority.

[54] Gurchiek, K. (2021, March 1). *Inclusive Strategies Create a 'More Universal Workplace'.* Society of Human Resources Management. www.shrm.org/resourcesandtools/hr-topics/behavioral-competencies/global-and-cultural-effectiveness/pages/inclusive-strategies-create-a-more-universal-workplace-.aspx.

[55] Tappe, A. (2019, October 21). *JPMorgan wants to hire people with criminal backgrounds | CNN Business.* CNN. www.cnn.com/2019/10/21/business/jpmorgan-criminal-record-jobs/index.html. ttps://www.cnn.com/2019/10/21/business/jpmorgan-criminal-record-jobs/index.html

[56] Peters, A. (2020, February 11). *The Body Shop will start hiring the first person who applies for any retail job.* Fast Company. www.fastcompany.com/90462746/the-body-shop-will-start-hiring-the-first-person-who-applies-for-any-retail-job.

[57] Greyston Center for Open Hiring. www.greyston.org/about-the-greyston-center-for-open-hiring.

[58] Pinkus, E. (2020). *Living Corporate poll: Candidate experience.* SurveyMonkey. www.surveymonkey.com/curiosity/living-corporate-poll-candidate-experience.

[59] Stripe (2021). *stripe.com/jobs.*

CHAPTER 4:
Start Me Up: Promoting Diversity

[60] *Women in the Workplace 2019: The State of Women in Corporate America.* Lean In. leanin.org/women-in-the-workplace-2019.

[61] Elsesser, K. (2019, October 16). *New LeanIn Study: The Broken Rung Keeping Women From Management.* Forbes. www.forbes.com/sites/kimelsesser/2019/10/15/new-leanin-study-the-broken-rung-keeping-women-from-management/?sh=7dbba9707803.

[62] Spary, S. (2021, May 12). *Unilever achieves 50/50 gender balance across global leadership.* Campaign. www.campaignlive.co.uk/article/unilever-achieves-50-50-gender-balance-across-global-leadership/1675761.

[63] Lock, S. (2019, June 24). *Baker McKenzie Sets Six-Year Target For Gender Diversity.* Law.com. www.law.com/international-edition/2019/06/24/baker-mckenzie-sets-six-year-target-for-gender-diversity.

[64] Hahm, M. (2018, March 21). *Half of Target's 1,800 stores are led by women.* Yahoo! www.yahoo.com/entertainment/half-targets-1800-stores-led-women-174835707.html.

[65] *Unilever achieves gender balance across management globally.* (2020) Unilever global company website. www.unilever.com/news/press-releases/2020/unilever-achieves-gender-balance-across-management-globally.html.

[66] Elsesser, K. (2019, October 16). *New LeanIn Study: The Broken Rung Keeping Women From Management.* Forbes. www.forbes.com/sites/kimelsesser/2019/10/15/new-leanin-study-the-broken-rung-keeping-women-from-management.

[67] *Sponsorship advances top talent, so why aren't we using it.* (2016). Deloitte. www2.deloitte.com/content/dam/Deloitte/ca/Documents/human-capital/ca-en-diversahack-report.pdf.

[68] *The Sponsor Dividend.* (2019). Coqual. www.talentinnovation.org/_private/assets/TheSponsorDividend_KeyFindingsCombined-CTI.pdf

[69] *corporate responsibility.* Target Corporate. (2017). corporate.target.com/corporate-responsibility.

[70] Kramer, J., McNamara, S., & Keenan, D. *Best Practices for Sponsorship Programs.* Diversity Best Practices. www.diversitybestpractices.com/best-practices-for-sponsorship-programs.

[71] Anderson, B. *How a Diversity Scorecard Helps Salesforce Keep Equality Top of Mind for Its Leaders.* Business Solutions on LinkedIn. business.linkedin.com/talent-solutions/blog/diversity/2019/why-salesforce-created-diversity-scorecard.

[72] *Lesbians Who Tech (Not IRL)* Pride Summit 2021, June 21st - June 25th. Lesbians Who Tech & Allies. (2021, June 22). lesbianswhotech.org/pridesummit2021.

[73] Wigder, Z. (2020, January 30). *Shoptalk doesn't have the best female speakers – we have the best speakers. Full stop.* Shoptalk.com shoptalk.com/blog/shoptalk-doesnt-have-the-best-female-speakers-we-have-the-best-speakers-full-stop.

[74] Bernstein, L. (2019, June 12) *NIH Director will no longer speak on all male science panels.* Washington Post. www.washingtonpost.com/health/nih-director-will-no-longer-speak-on-all-male-science-panels/2019/06/12/fe3b6386-8d2c-11e9-adf3-f70f78c156e8_story.html.

[75] *Withdrawal from Speaking at PHPCE 2019.* Mark Baker's Blog. (2019, July 24). markbakeruk.net/2019/07/24/withdrawal-from-speaking-at-phpce-2019.

CHAPTER 5:
True Colors: Every Voice Matters

[76] Brown, D. (2020, February 5). *A Starbucks ad that matters: Coffee brand shows how important names are for trans people.* USA Today. www.usatoday.com/story/tech/2020/02/05/touching-starbucks-ad-spotlights-transgender-person-trying-new-name/4665116002.

[77] Kim, A. (2019, September 27). *The world's first transgender professional boxer is now the face of Everlast.* CNN. edition.cnn.com/2019/09/27/sport/transgender-boxer-everlast-trnd/index.html.

[78] Guardian News and Media. (2019, June 19). *Unilever boss says brands using 'woke-washing' destroy trust.* The Guardian. www.theguardian.com/media/2019/jun/19/unilever-boss-says-brands-using-woke-washing-destroy-trust.

[79] Beer, J. (2019, September 24). *17,000 data points from 50 top brands prove that diversity in ads is good for their bottom lines.* Fast Company. www.fastcompany.com/90407174/diversity-advertising-good-brands-bottom-line.

[80] Peck, E. (2016, December 12). *What Happened When One CEO Decided To Talk Openly About Race.* HuffPost. www.huffpost.com/entry/workplace-diversity-pwc_n_584af4fbe4b0bd9c3dfc976b.

[81] Moore, P., Graham, L., Hutchinson, A., & Huber, M. F. (2021, June 27). *Why Altra Signing Two Pregnant Runners Is a Big Deal*. Outside Online. www.outsideonline.com/2409180/altra-pregnant-runners-alysia-montano-tina-muir.

[82] Dixon, E. (2019, June 6). *Nike introduces plus-size mannequins to London store*. CNN. www.cnn.com/style/article/london-nike-mannequins-scli-intl/index.html.

[83] Zanger. (2019, June 19). *'The Talk' Makes Way for 'The Look' in Powerful New P&G Ad Addressing Race in America*. Adweek. www.adweek.com/brand-marketing/the-talk-makes-way-for-the-look-in-powerful-new-pg-ad-addressing-race-in-america.

[84] *"Queer in Tech" free stock photos*. (2021, July 20). Mapbox. www.flickr.com/photos/mapbox/albums/72157713100349311.

[85] The Gender Spectrum Collection by Broadly. genderphotos.vice.com/.

[86] Beautifully Diverse Stock Photos. Nappy. nappy.co/.

[87] Heasley, S. (2020, January 10). *American Girl Introduces Doll With Disability*. Disability Scoop. www.disabilityscoop.com/2020/01/10/american-girl-introduces-doll-with-disability/27632.

[88] Guardian News and Media. (2019, October 10). *Sesame Street takes on opioids crisis as muppet's mother battles addiction*. The Guardian. www.theguardian.com/tv-and-radio/2019/oct/09/sesame-street-karli-addiction-opioids-crisis.

[89] Dockterman, E., Bakalar, S., & Tsai, D. (2019, September 25). *Why Mattel Is Releasing the First Gender-Neutral Doll*. Time. time.com/5684822/mattel-gender-neutral-doll/.

[90] Beresford, T. (2019, November 14). *GLAAD, Microsoft Collaborate on Major Playable Transgender Game Character*. The Hollywood Reporter. www.hollywoodreporter.com/movies/movie-news/glaad-microsoft-collaborate-major-playable-transgender-game-character-1254411.

[91] McCauley, M. C. (2019, November 20). *Baltimore Museum of Art will only acquire works from women next year: 'You have to do something radical'*. baltimoresun.com. www.baltimoresun.com/entertainment/arts/bs-fe-bma-female-artists-2020-20191115-33s5hjjnqfghzhmwkt7dqbargq-story.html.

[92] *SFMOMA Sells Rothko Painting To Fund Purchase Of 11 Works … sfist*. com/2019/06/28/sfmoma-sells-rothko-painting-to-fund-purchase-of-works-by-women-and-minorities.

[93] *Limbong, A. Country Music Channel Promises Equal Video Plays … - NPR.org*. www.npr.org/2020/01/21/798193382/country-music-channel-promises-equal-video-plays-for-women-and-men.

[94] All Things Considered. (2020, December 22). *'Kansas City Star' Publishes Apology For Its Coverage Of Black Community*. www.npr.org/2020/12/22/949309308/kansas-city-star-publishes-apology-for-its-coverage-of-black-community.

[95] Alicandri, J. (2020, November 20). *IBM apologizes For Firing Computer Pioneer For Being Transgender…52 Years Later*. Forbes. www.forbes.com/sites/jeremyalicandri/2020/11/18/ibm-apologizes-for-firing-computer-pioneer.

[96] Asmelash, L. (2020, June 25). *NASA will name its headquarters after Mary W. Jackson, the agency's first African American female engineer*. CNN. www.cnn.com/2020/06/25/us/mary-w-jackson-hidden-figures-nasa-building-trnd/index.html.

CHAPTER 6:
Sign O' the Times: Understanding Equity

[97] Person. (2020, December 16). *MLB officially designates the Negro Leagues as 'Major League'*. MLB.com. www.mlb.com/press-release/press-release-mlb-officially-designates-the-negro-leagues-as-major-league.

[98] Stahl, A. (2020, July 21). *10 Steps Businesses Can Take to Improve Diversity and Inclusion in the Workforce*. Forbes. www.forbes.com/sites/ashleystahl/2020/07/21/10-steps-businesses-can-take-to-improve-diversity-and-inclusion-in-the-workforce/#3e75ac-3b343e.

[99] *Our Work*. Movement Advancement Project |. www.lgbtmap.org.

CHAPTER 7:
What's Going On: Racial Justice

[100] *Disparities in Wealth by Race and Ethnicity in the 2019 Survey of Consumer Finances*. (2019). The Fed - Disparities in Wealth by Race and Ethnicity in the 2019 Survey of Consumer Finances. www.federalreserve.gov/econres/notes/feds-notes/dispari-ties-in-wealth-by-Antiracism Center.

[101] www.ibramxkendi.com/antiracism-center-2.

[102] Thomas, E. (2020, June 2). *Why CEO Black Lives Matter Communications Are Critical: A DIBs Leader's Perspective: Upwork*. RSS. www.upwork.com/resources/why-ceo-black-lives-matter-communications-are-critical-dibs-leader-perspective.

[103] *Silence Is NOT An Option*. Ben and Jerry's. www.benjerry.com/about-us/media-cen-ter/dismantle-white-supremacy.

[104] Mulqueen, T. (2021, January 20). *Brands Want to Tell Stories of Inclusion. Marketing Leaders Should Listen Instead*. Entrepreneur. www.entrepreneur.com/article/362561.

[105] Lim, C.-J. (2019, December 5). *Pinterest And The Knot Will Stop Promoting Wedding Content That Romanticizes Former Slave Plantations*. BuzzFeed News. www.buzzfeed-news.com/article/clarissajanlim/plantation-weddings-pinterest-knot.

CHAPTER 8:
RESPECT.: Equitable Pay

[106] Brown, Riva. WPSU - Penn State Public Media. *Case Study: H&M's Coolest Mon-key in the Jungle*. www.pagecentertraining.psu.edu/public-relations-ethics/introduc-tion-to-diversity-and-public-relations/lesson-2-how-to-reach-diverse-stakeholders/reaching-diverse-stakeholders-externally.

[107] Equal Pay Today! www.equalpaytoday.org.

[108] Gruver, J. (2020, June 17). *Racial Wage Gap for Men - Compensation Research*. Pay-Scale. www.payscale.com/data/racial-wage-gap-for-men.

[109] *Gender Pay Gap Shortchanges Women $500 Billion Annually*. AAUW. (2020, March 10). www.aauw.org/resources/news/media/press-releases/gender-pay-gap-shortchang-es-women-500-billion-annually.

[110] Jackson, S. NBC News (2019, December 17). *It will be 257 years before women have equal pay, gender gap report says*. www.nbcnews.com/news/world/it-will-be-257-years-women-have-equal-pay-new-n1103481.

[111] Tornone, K. (2018, December 20). *A running list of states and localities that have outlawed pay history questions*. HR Dive. www.hrdive.com/news/salary-histo-ry-ban-states-list/516662.

[112] Leonhardt, M. CNBC news. (2020, January 31) *60% of women say they've never negotiated their salary—and many quit their job instead.* www.cnbc.com/2020/01/31/women-more-likely-to-change-jobs-to-get-pay-increase.html.

[113] Asmelash, L. CNN. (2019, September 10). *In the new game of Monopoly, women make more than men.* www.cnn.com/2019/09/10/us/hasbro-ms-monopoly-trnd/index.html?.

[114] March 9, 2020. (2020, September 18). *2020 Salesforce Equal Pay Update.* Salesforce News. www.salesforce.com/news/stories/2020-salesforce-equal-pay-update.

[115] Lyft, I. *Lyft's 2020 Pay Equity Audit.* Lyft. www.lyft.com/blog/posts/our-ongoing-commitment-to-pay-fairness.

[116] McGrath, M. (2019, July 31). *Lyft's 2019 Pay Equity Audit Has A Surprising Result: Its Male And Female Employees Earn The Same Thing.* Forbes. www.forbes.com/sites/maggiemcgrath/2019/07/31/lyfts-2019-pay-equity-audit-has-a-surprising-result-its-male-and-female-employees-earn-the-same-thing/?sh=1e2d92d67a8d.

[117] Bolden-Barrett, V. (2019, August 13). *Nordstrom says it reached 100% pay equity across gender and race.* HR Dive. www.hrdive.com/news/nordstrom-says-it-reached-100-pay-equity-across-gender-and-race/560643.

[118] Press, The Canadian. (2019, December 1). *Brier and Tournament of Hearts reach pay equity for 2020 curling championships.* thestar.com. www.thestar.com/sports/curling/2019/12/01/brier-and-tournament-of-hearts-reach-pay-equity-for-2020-curling-championships.html.

[119] Banjo, S. (2020, August 27). *One Easy Way to Close the Gender Pay Gap.* Bloomberg. www.bloomberg.com/news/newsletters/2020-08-27/bloomberg-equality-one-easy-way-to-close-the-gender-pay-gap.

[120] Herbst, J. (2021, January 27). *Why we adjusted salaries for all traditionally female-dominated roles at our company.* Fast Company. www.fastcompany.com/90597793/why-we-adjusted-salaries-for-all-traditionally-female-dominated-roles-at-our-company.

[121] *Minimum Wage.* United States Department of Labor. www.dol.gov/agencies/whd/minimum-wage.

[122] *Living Wage calculator.* Living Wage Calculator. livingwage.mit.edu/articles/61-new-living-wage-data-for-now-available-on-the-tool.

[123] Redman, R. (2020, April 2). *Walmart invests $550M, Target $300M in employees on coronavirus front lines.* Supermarket News. www.supermarketnews.com/retail-financial/walmart-invests-550m-target-300m-employees-coronavirus-front-lines.

[124] Qiao, J. (2019, August 7). *Fifth Third is latest bank to raise its minimum wage.* American Banker. www.americanbanker.com/news/fifth-third-is-latest-bank-to-raise-its-minimum-wage.

[125] *Bank of America Accelerates Move to $20 per Hour Minimum Wage.* newsroom.bankofamerica.com/press-releases/corporate-and-financial-news/bank-america-accelerates-move-20-hour-minimum-wage-2020.

[126] Kelly, J. (2021, January 8). *Why Delta Air Lines' $1.6 Billion Bonus Payout To Employees Is A Smart Business Decision.* Forbes. www.forbes.com/sites/jackkelly/2020/01/23/why-delta-air-lines-16-billion-bonus-payout-to-employees-is-a-smart-business-decision.

[127] Clarke, C. (2019, December 11). *Real estate company gives employees $10 million holiday bonus: "Totally blown away".* CBS News. www.cbsnews.com/news/maryland-real-estate-company-gifts-its-employees-10-million-bonus-st-john-properties-christmas.

[128] Draznin, H. (2020, January 6). *Eileen Fisher built a fashion empire. Her employees now own nearly half of it.* CNN. www.cnn.com/2020/01/06/success/eileen-fisher-profit-sharing-fashion-boss-files/index.html.

[129] *Stock & Dividend Information.* Publix Super Markets. www.publixstockholder.com/stock-and-dividend-information.

CHAPTER 9:
Money! Money! Money! Equitable Spend and Access

[130] *CVS Health Supplier Diversity Impact Report 2019.* cvshealth.com/sites/default/files/cvs-health-supplier-diversity-impact-report-2019.pdf.

[131] *External Supplier Diversity Quick Start Guide.* (2020). Semi Worldwide. semi.org/sites/semi.org/files/2020-01/external-supplier-diversity-quick-start-guide.pdf.

[132] Dobrosielski, C. (2019, June 27). *Marriott to spend $500M with women-owned businesses in 2019.* Hotel Management. www.hotelmanagement.net/own/marriott-to-spend-500m-women-owned-businesses-2019.

[133] *An open letter on requiring diversity from our vendors & partners.* SurveyMonkey. www.surveymonkey.com/curiosity/an-open-letter-on-requiring-diversity-from-our-vendors-partners.

[134] Rodgers, S. (2019, November 21). *The Intel Rule: Action to Improve Diversity in the Legal Profession.* Intel. newsroom.intel.com/editorials/intel-rule-action-improve-diversity-legal-profession. ttps://newsroom.intel.com/editorials/intel-rule-action-improve-diversity-legal-profession/

[135] Cassens Weiss, D. (2017, May 17). *HP General Counsel Tells Law Firms to Meet Diversity Mandate or Forfeit Up to 10 Percent of Fees.* American Bar Association. www.americanbar.org/groups/litigation/committees/diversity-inclusion/articles/2017/spring2017-0517-hp-general-counsel-diversity-mandate.

[136] Cassens Weiss, D. (2021, January 28). *Coca-Cola General Counsel Gests Tough with Law Firms that Fail to Meet Diversity Goals.* ABA Journal Publication. www.abajournal.com/news/article/coca-cola-general-counsel-gets-tough-with-law-firms-that-fai-to-meet-diversity-goals.

[137] Troise, D., & Olson, A. (2018, February 25). Associated Press. *More companies end ties with NRA as pressure mounts.* apnews.com/article/8f9b585f1a1f449ca-36e4469566767ad.

[138] Gandel, S. (2019, November 27). *Charles Schwab charitable fund halts donations to NRA.* CBS News. www.cbsnews.com/news/charles-schwab-charitable-fund-halts-donations-to-nra.

[139] *Edelman Trust Barometer 2020.* www.edelman.com/trust/2020-trust-barometer.

[140] *15 Percent Pledge.* www.15percentpledge.org/.

[141] Sahadi, J. (2020, September 16). *This Shark Tank star is partnering with Lowe's to help minority-owned businesses.* CNN. www.cnn.com/2020/09/15/success/lowes-daymond-john-minority-entrepreneurs/index.html.

[142] *Groceries, Pharmacy, Pickup and Delivery.* (2020, December 21). Giant Food. giantfood.com/pages/giant-food-introduces-shelf-labels-to-spotlight-products-owned-by-minority-buisnesses.

[143] www.target.com/c/black-owned-or-founded-brands-at-target/-/N-q8v16
[144] Associated Press. (2020, June 11). *Walmart, CVS, Walgreens to stop locking up black beauty products.* www.marketwatch.com/story/walmart-cvs-walgreens-to-stop-locking-up-black-beauty-products-2020-06-11?

[145] Connley, C. Classicalycourt. (2020, October 8). *Black and Latinx founders have received just 2.6% of VC funding so far in 2020, according to new report.* CNBC. www.cnbc.com/2020/10/07/black-and-latinx-founders-have-received-just-2point6percent-of-vc-funding-in-2020-so-far.html.

[146] Liu, S., & Parilla, J. (2020, June 17). *Businesses owned by women and minorities have grown. Will COVID-19 undo that?* Brookings. www.brookings.edu/research/businesses-owned-by-women-and-minorities-have-grown-will-covid-19-undo-that.

[147] Decker, M. (2021, February 10). *Meet The BIPOC-Owned Brands Launching At Sephora In 2021.* Sephora Accelerate Program Full List 2021 BIPOC Brands. www.refinery29.com/en-us/2021/02/10302693/sephora-accelerate-bipoc-brands-2021.

[148] Callahan, C. (2020, June 18). *How ThirdLove is helping businesses owned by women of color.* Yahoo! news.yahoo.com/thirdlove-giving-back-female-entrepreneurs-195336613.html.

[149] *Constellation Brands Announces Comprehensive Effort in Advancing Social Justice and Eliminating Systemic Racism.* (2020, June 29). Constellation Brands. www.cbrands.com/news/articles/constellation-brands-announces-comprehensive-effort-in-advancing-social-justice-and-eliminating-systemic-racism.

[150] *Target Commits $10 Million and Ongoing Resources for Rebuilding Efforts and Advancing Social Justice.* (2020, June 5). Target Corporate. corporate.target.com/article/2020/06/commitments-rebuilding-and-social-justice.

[151] Shaw, L., & Bloomberg. (2020, July 2). *Netflix will move $100 million into Black-owned banks.* Fortune. fortune.com/2020/06/30/netflix-100-million-black-owned-banks.

CHAPTER 10:
Come Together: Understanding Inclusion

[152] Riggio, O. (2020, August 4). *Exploring the History and Evolution of Employee Resource Groups.* DiversityInc. www.diversityinc.com/history-and-evolution-of-employee-resource-groups-ergs.

[153] *Stepping Up the Fight Against Discrimination.* (2019, October 14). Whirlpool. www.pressreleasepoint.com/stepping-fight-against-discrimination.

CHAPTER 11:
Just the Way You Are: Inclusive Conversations

[154] Hallinger, N. Linkedin. www.linkedin.com/posts/nhallinger_democrats-behaviorchange-uselection-activity-6731422004739682304-eT5c.

[155] *A quote by Maya Angelou.* Goodreads. www.goodreads.com/quotes/5934-i-ve-learned-that-people-will-forget-what-you-said-people.

[156] Smith, C., & Yoshino, K. (2019). *Uncovering Talent: A New Model of Inclusion.* Deloitte. www2.deloitte.com/content/dam/Deloitte/us/Documents/about-deloitte/us-about-deloitte-uncovering-talent-a-new-model-of-inclusion.pdf.

[157] Fearless Organization. www.fearlessorganization.com.

[158] Duhigg, C. (2016, February 25). *What Google Learned From Its Quest to Build the Perfect Team.* The New York Times. www.nytimes.com/2016/02/28/magazine/what-google-learned-from-its-quest-to-build-the-perfect-team.html.

[159] Braswell, P. (2021, January 27). *Delta's CEO Ed Bastian: Taking a Stand on Racial Equity.* Harvard Business Review. hbr.org/podcast/2021/01/deltas-ceo-ed-bastian-taking-a-stand-on-racial-equity.

[160] Jenkins, C. (2020, December 11). *Fauci addresses Black Americans' vaccine concerns: This was 'developed by an African American woman'.* TheHill. thehill.com/homenews/news/529841-fauci-addresses-black-americans-vaccine-concerns-this-was-developed-by-an.

[161] Robison, J. (2021, May 25). *How The Ritz-Carlton Manages the Mystique.* Gallup. news.gallup.com/businessjournal/112906/how-ritzcarlton-manages-mystique.aspx.

[162] Compton, J. (2019, December 28). *More LGBTQ millennials plan to have kids regardless of income, survey finds.* NBC News. www.nbcnews.com/feature/nbc-out/more-lgbtq-millennials-plan-have-kids-regardless-income-survey-finds-n1107461.

[163] Compton, J. (2019, February 7). *LGBTQ families poised for 'dramatic growth,' national survey finds.* NBC News. www.nbcnews.com/feature/nbc-out/lgbtq-families-poised-dramatic-growth-national-survey-finds-n968776.

[164] *Secretary of State Alex Padilla Partners with Equality California Institute to Protect Voting Rights of Transgender Californians in 2020.* (2020). www.sos.ca.gov/administration/news-releases-and-advisories/2019-news-releases-and-advisories/secretary-state-alex-padilla-partners-equality-california-institute-protect-voting-rights-transgender-californians-2020.

[165] Mena, K. (2019, December 12). *New York wants taxi drivers to be aware of pronouns and how to use them | CNN Politics.* CNN. www.cnn.com/2019/12/12/politics/nyc-taxi-commission-pronoun-guidance-email/index.html.

[166] BBC. (2018, September 6). *Trans woman's bank account frozen in 'sounded like man' row.* BBC News. www.bbc.com/news/uk-england-nottinghamshire-45406917.

CHAPTER 12:
Express Yourself:
Inclusive Employee Benefits and Expression

[167] Mullen, C. (2020, January). *Gen Buy: Millennials projected to spend $1.4 trillion as influence grows.* The Business Journals. www.bizjournals.com/bizwomen/news/latest-news/2020/01/gen-buymillennials-projected-to-spend-1-4-trillion.html?page=all.

[168] Kurter, H. (2019, June 23). *Companies Striving For Diversity And Inclusion Are Rethinking Their Dress Code Policy.* Forbes. www.forbes.com/sites/heidilynnekurter/2019/06/23/2-simple-ways-to-cultivate-a-culture-of-diversity-and-inclusion-through-self-expression/?sh=628c6e1610af

[169] *KWANZAA - December 26, 2021.* National Today. (2021, June 4). nationaltoday.com/kwanzaa.

[170] Dzhanova, Y. (2020, June 19). *Here's a running list of all the big companies observing Juneteenth this year.* CNBC. www.cnbc.com/2020/06/17/here-are-the-companies-observing-juneteenth-this-year.html.

[171] Livingston, G., & Thomas, D. (2020, August 7). *Among 41 countries, only U.S. lacks paid parental leave.* Pew Research Center. www.pewresearch.org/fact-tank/2019/12/16/u-s-lacks-mandated-paid-parental-leave.

[172] *Oregon Family Leave Act (OFLA).* BOLI : Oregon Family Leave Act (OFLA) : For Workers : State of Oregon. www.oregon.gov/boli/workers/pages/oregon-family-leave.aspx.

[173] Scott, S., & Wheatley, A. (2019, July 16). *Oregon Passes Nation's Most Generous Paid Family Leave Law.* Society of Human Resources Management. www.shrm.org/resourcesandtools/legal-and-compliance/state-and-local-updates/pages/oregon-passes-generous-paid-family-leave-law.aspx.

[174] Molla, R. (2018, January 31). *Netflix parents get a paid year off and Amazon pays for spouses' parental leave.* Vox. www.vox.com/2018/1/31/16944976/new-parents-tech-companies-google-hp-facebook-twitter-netflix.

[175] Todd, S. *Sweetgreen's emergency fund helps its lowest-wage workers cope with crises.* Quartz. qz.com/work/1648042/sweetgreen-employees-contribute-to-a-worker-emergency-fund.

[176] Cheng, M. (2019, June 10). *Target is expanding parental leave, including for hourly and part-time workers.* Quartz. qz.com/work/1640142/target-expands-parental-leave-and-other-benefits-for-hourly-and-part-time-workers.

[177] Hudson, C. (2020, December 16). *Bank of America extends child-care benefits through the first quarter.* The Business Journals. www.bizjournals.com/charlotte/news/2020/12/16/bank-of-america-child-care-benefits-extended-again.html.

[178] Hinchliffe, E. (2020, September 14). *The best back-to-school benefits companies are offering their employees.* Fortune. fortune.com/2020/09/10/back-to-school-benefits-discounts-parents-caregivers/.

[179] Mayer, K. (2020, September 4). *How KPMG is boosting its support of working parents.* Human Resources Executive. hrexecutive.com/how-kpmg-is-boosting-its-support-of-working-parents.

[180] Mayer, K. (2020, May 7). *Target updates paid leave benefits in wake of coronavirus.* Human Resources Executive. hrexecutive.com/target-updates-benefits-in-wake-of-coronavirus.

[181] McGregor, J. (2019, April 7). *The newest benefit for working moms.* The Washington Post. www.washingtonpost.com/news/on-leadership/wp/2015/08/18/the-newest-benefit-for-working-moms-paying-for-a-nanny-on-business-trips.

[182] *Human Rights Campaign Foundation Announces New Corporate Equality Index Criteria.* HRC. www.hrc.org/press-releases/human-rights-campaign-foundation-announces-new-corporate-equality-index-cri.

[183] Clarey, K. (2019, March 18). *How workplace chaplains are giving Tyson Foods a major assist.* HR Dive. www.hrdive.com/news/how-workplace-chaplains-are-giving-tyson-foods-a-major-assist/550599.

[184] Green, L. (2020, February 26). *Religion in the workplace good for business, Tyson Foods high on the list.* Fox News. www.foxnews.com/faith-values/religion-in-the-workplace-good-for-business-tyson-foods-high-on-the-list.

[185] Vasel, K. (2019, May 23). *Intel was losing employees. So it created an anonymous hotline to help unhappy workers.* CNN. www.cnn.com/2019/05/23/success/intel-warmline-employee-retention/index.html.

[186] Barber, K. (2021, January 22). *Why publishers are adding benefits to lift employee peace of mind.* Digiday. digiday.com/media/not-just-the-zoom-happy-hour-how-publishers-are-adding-benefits-to-lift-employee-peace-of-mind.

[187] Levy, A. (2020, October 11). *Companies are offering benefits like virtual therapy and meditation apps as Covid-19 stress grows.* CNBC. www.cnbc.com/2020/10/10/covid-stress-companies-turn-to-virtual-therapy-meditation-apps.html.

[188] Good, B. (2021, July 28). *Walmart Tests New Employee Retention Strategy.* DiversityInc. www.diversityinc.com/walmart-tests-new-employee-retention-strategy-by-covering-100-of-college-tuition-fees/.

[189] Hess, A. (2019, October 21). *Chipotle is the latest company to spend millions on this expensive benefit for its employees-here's why.* CNBC. www.cnbc.com/2019/10/18/chipotle-employees-can-go-to-college-debt-free.html.

[190] Toh, M., & Wakatsuki, Y. (2019, November 18). *Microsoft tried a 4-day workweek in Japan. Productivity jumped 40%.* CNN. www.cnn.com/2019/11/04/tech/microsoft-japan-workweek-productivity/index.html.

[191] Noguchi, Y. (2015, April 18). *Enjoy the Extra Day Off*. Houston Public Media. www.houstonpublicmedia.org/npr/2020/02/21/807133509/enjoy-the-extra-day-off-more-bosses-give-4-day-workweek-a-try.

[192] Bank of America *careers.bankofamerica.com/en-us/culture/diversity-inclusion/veterans*

[193] *LGBTQs Are a $1 Trillion Opportunity for Companies, Says Brand-New Study*. (2018, August 2). Hornet. hornet.com/about/queer-people-hornet-kantar.

[194] Turner, N. (2019, November 6). *T-Mobile lets retail staff add their pronouns to name tags*. Bloomberg. www.bloomberg.com/news/articles/2019-11-06/t-mobile-lets-retail-staff-add-their-pronouns-to-name-tags.

[195] Fessler, L. (2018, April 3). *GM's dress code is only two words*. Yahoo! finance.yahoo.com/news/gm-dress-code-only-two-110326859.html.

[196] Brito, C. (2019, March 4). *Virgin Atlantic gets rid of mandatory makeup rules for female cabin crew*. CBS News. www.cbsnews.com/news/virgin-atlantic-makeup-female-cabin-crew-members-cosmetics.

[197] BBC. (2019, June 4). *Mexico City drops gender-specific school uniforms*. www.bbc.com/news/world-latin-america-48511416.

[198] Halzack, S. (2018, June 10). *Target to spend $20 million to add single-stall bathrooms at stores*. chicagotribune.com. www.chicagotribune.com/business/ct-target-earnings-20160817-story.html.

[199] Burns, K. (2020, October 27). Twitter. twitter.com/kamcburns/status/1173964765636550656.

[200] Bologna, C. *Ashton Kutcher Continues Fight For Dads' Rights To Change Diapers With Online Petition*. Huff Post. www.huffpost.com/entry/ashton-kutcher-chan-georg-petition-changing-tables_n_6933100.

[201] Duhigg, C. (2016, February 25). *What Google Learned From Its Quest to Build the Perfect Team*. The New York Times. www.nytimes.com/2016/02/28/magazine/what-google-learned-from-its-quest-to-build-the-perfect-team.html.

CHAPTER 13:
9 to 5: Random Acts of Inclusion

[202] *Our Work*. Movement Advancement Project. www.lgbtmap.org.

[203] Johnson, W., al., D. K. et, & Daimler, M. (2019, December 16). *The Value of Belonging at Work*. Harvard Business Review. hbr.org/2019/12/the-value-of-belonging-at-work.

[204] Byers, D. (2020, May 13). *Twitter employees can work from home forever, CEO says*. NBC News. www.nbcnews.com/tech/tech-news/twitter-employees-can-work-home-forever-ceo-says-n1205346.

[205] Schneider, J. 2019, October 15). *A restaurant with an autism-friendly sensory room is opening in N.J.* NJ.com. www.nj.com/food/2019/10/a-restaurant-with-an-autism-friendly-sensory-room-is-opening-in-nj.html

[206] Lewis, S. (2019, July 19). *Target introduces adaptive Halloween costumes for kids with disabilities*. CBS News. www.cbsnews.com/news/target-introduces-adaptive-halloween-costumes-for-kids-with-disabilities.

[207] Garrand, D. (2019, October 2). *Mattel debuts first official Braille deck of UNO cards*. CBS News. www.cbsnews.com/news/uno-card-mattel-debuts-first-official-braille-deck-of-uno-cards.

[208] Kaplan, J. (2020, January 9). *Google Reveals 2,000-Person Diversity And Inclusion Product Team.* Digital Trends. www.digitaltrends.com/news/google-diversity-inclusion-champions-announcement-ces-2020.

[209] Kim, S. (2019, December 3). *Comcast Now Offers Customer Service In ASL, A First For The Cable Industry.* Forbes. www.forbes.com/sites/sarahkim/2019/12/03/comcast-asl-now.

[210] Grothaus, M. (2017, September 29). *Uber is now offering sign language tips to riders with deaf drivers.* Fast Company. www.fastcompany.com/40474992/uber-is-now-offering-sign-language-tips-to-riders-with-deaf-drivers.

[211] Ennis, D. (2019, December 8). *Thanks To Mastercard, Everyone Can Now Get A Card With Their True Name.* Forbes. www.forbes.com/sites/dawnstaceyennis/2019/11/29/thanks-to-mastercard-this-is-the-last-black-friday-you-cant-use-your-true-name.

CHAPTER 14:
Voices Carry: Allyship in Action

[212] Korver, K. (2019, April 8). *Privileged: By Kyle Korver.* The Players' Tribune. www.theplayerstribune.com/articles/kyle-korver-utah-jazz-nba.

[213] Jana, T., & Baran, Michael. (2020) *Subtle Acts of Exclusion.*

[214] Dwyer, C. (2019, December 10). *Merriam-Webster Singles Out Nonbinary 'They' For Word Of The Year Honors.* National Public Radio. www.npr.org/2019/12/10/786732456/merriam-webster-singles-out-nonbinary-they-for-word-of-the-year-honors.

[215] American Psychological Association. *Bias-free language.* apastyle.apa.org/style-grammar-guidelines/bias-free-language.

[216] *A brief history of singular 'they'.* (2019, March 29). Oxford English Dictionary. public.oed.com/blog/a-brief-history-of-singular-they.

[217] Crocker, B. (2019, June 21). *Cracker Barrel CEO Sandra Cochran leads charge for chain's racial, LGBTQ inclusivity.* Knoxville News Sentinel. www.knoxnews.com/story/news/2019/06/21/grayston-fitts-controversy-highlights-cracker-barrel-advances-on-diversity-inclusivity/1498513001.

[218] Hauer, S. (2020, August 28). *Penzeys Spices wants to 'loot' its Kenosha store in support of protests.* Milwaukee Journal Sentinel. www.jsonline.com/story/money/business/2020/08/28/penzeys-spices-wants-loot-kenosha-store-support-protests/5655874002.

[219] *Tapestry shines a spotlight on diversity.* (2019, September 6). Yahoo! news.yahoo.com/tapestry-shines-spotlight-diversity-130221634.html.

[220] McGregor, J. (2019, April 7). *Anatomy of a PR response: How Starbucks is handling its Philadelphia crisis.* The Washington Post. www.washingtonpost.com/news/on-leadership/wp/2018/04/19/anatomy-of-a-pr-response-how-starbucks-is-handling-its-philadelphia-crisis/.

EPILOGUE:
Don't Stop Believin': Understanding Belonging

[221] Wikimedia Foundation. (2021, July 18). *The Hill We Climb.* Wikipedia. en.wikipedia.org/wiki/The_Hill_We_Climb.

Index

About the Author

BERNADETTE SMITH is Founder and CEO of the Equality Institute and an IBPA Benjamin Franklin booksellers Gold medal award-winning author of three books on LGBTQ inclusion. She is frequently requested as a keynote speaker to help promote an inclusive work environment and celebrate diversity. She has consulted with Fortune 500 companies and presented to a variety of audiences, including CEOs, leadership teams, human resource and diversity leaders, sales and marketing professionals and more.

Because of her insight and impact as a change agent, she has been featured in the New York Times, USA Today, the Washington Post, and Fast Company. She's appeared on CNN, the Today Show, the BBC, and National Public Radio. Bernadette has been named one of Chicago's Notable LGBTQ Executives by Crain's Chicago Business.

9 781737 635413